A CHILLING SELF-PORTRAIT

Arthur Bremer had nothing against the men he tried to kill. He simply had a desperate desire to be "somebody."

And to make sure his name went in the history books, he wrote down his inmost thoughts and observations as he prepared for the crime.

This chilling diary takes you through six unsuccessful attempts on President Nixon's life to within a few days of Bremer's shooting of Alabama Governor George Wallace. It chronicles the desperation of an utterly "ordinary" American—young, unemployed, frustrated in love, nagged by feelings of inadequacy and insignificance. It is a pathetic, contemporary story—and an ominous document that will make you tremble for the safety of our nation's leaders.

"Frustration fairly steams from these pages. ...Like many of our best writers, Bremer senses the madness, the absurdity of our world. We don't have to read far into [this book] to be chilled by its author's determination."   —*Newsweek*

AN ASSASSIN'S DIARY
was originally published by Harper's Magazine Press.

AN ASSASSIN'S DIARY

Arthur H. Bremer

Introduction by Harding Lemay

PUBLISHED BY POCKET BOOKS NEW YORK

AN ASSASSIN'S DIARY

Harper's Magazine Press edition published 1973

POCKET BOOK edition published October, 1973

"Harper's" is the registered trademark of Harper & Row, Publishers, Inc. Portions of this work first appeared in the January 1973 issue of **Harper's Magazine.**

This POCKET BOOK edition includes every word contained in the original, higher-priced edition. It is printed from brand-new plates made from completely reset, clear, easy-to-read type. POCKET BOOK editions are published by POCKET BOOKS, a division of Simon & Schuster, Inc., 630 Fifth Avenue, New York, N.Y. 10020. Trademarks registered in the United States and other countries.

L

Contents

Introduction

Thirteen diary entries, varying in length from half a page to nearly twenty and covering less than six weeks' time, can serve as a basis for nothing but speculation about the man who wrote them. That man, or rather that boy of twenty-two, is now locked away from the society that nurtured him, leaving behind these few scribbled pages and a crippled politician whose most potent appeal is to those who share the unarticulated rage that generated his would-be assassin. As Bremer himself remarks at one point, "Irony abounds."

Since I know practically nothing about Arthur H. Bremer beyond what his diary reveals, my speculations range from him to the society that has conditioned us both. His attitudes and responses to reality are colored and distorted by those influences that stain the perceptions of an entire population. Our experiences connect, and then diverge again, as I follow his. All twenty-one-year-old males drift along on eddies of ambitions, daydreams, and projective fantasies, or at least so it seems to me in recalling my own vagrant youth. At Bremer's age, I longed to leave behind (before going to an almost certain death in the Second World War) a name as easily recognizable as

Alfred Lunt's or Fredric March's. Theatrical celebrity was the extent of my hopes for renown, but for Bremer the stage is wider, as the dream is more intense. Accepting his own death as the penalty to be exacted, he convinced himself that future generations would remember his name as we remember John Wilkes Booth or Lee Harvey Oswald.

At twenty-one, also, knowledge of our fragile mortality wars with the juices racing through our bodies, and we are tossed back and forth between the mystery of each. These pages are a young man's diary, carelessly composed, punctuated by startling and sometimes touching flashes of the boy beneath the driven young man who ironically comments upon his obsession and yet cannot wrench himself free from it. The first half of the journal Arthur Bremer kept, which might reveal where and how he got the money which financed his activities, lies buried beyond the reach of authorities and speculation alike. We have only these handwritten pages found in his automobile after he shot Governor George Wallace in Maryland. Although Wallace was the final target of his ambition, the diary is devoted mostly to Bremer's futile efforts to kill President Nixon and thereby ensure himself instant renown in the newspapers and on television. His hopes for future renown appear to have been in the diary itself, which is a cry in the dark for recognition that he has existed in our midst.

Plans for assassinating the President are jumbled within a fabric of ordinary life in hotels, restaurants, on the streets, and in crowds welcoming

Nixon at airports or gathering to hear Wallace at a suburban rally. A compulsively written compendium of observations on people and places thrusts itself through the incoherent articulation of Bremer's preparations for an act he is totally unqualified to perform, and running through it all, like the current that supplies energy for life itself, is the urgency of sexual desire, only dimly understood by the man recording it so faithfully, recalling how he has been gulled by those who advertise fulfillment in the classified ads of the underground press. The man Bremer is shadowed throughout by the boy Bremer, innocently aping the activities of the beautiful killers on the television screens, those true heroes of a culture that escapes its common responsibility for a blood-drenched distant country by nightly immersion in the adventures of those who have guns and will travel.

While little in these pages is really alien to most of us, the record of daily expenses in hotels and the quality of food served in restaurants is so familiar that we glide over it without realizing that it is the clue to the mystery of Bremer's obsession. For he is afloat in a society in which every product has its list price and he practices comparison shopping as automatically as he breathes, right up to the choice of which target will provide him with the most lasting recognition. So he notes down everything, recalling price and quality for the necessities of life in the locales he haunts, waiting for his intended victim to walk into his trap. Occasionally, with unexpected sweetness, he notices the miracle of green grass thrusting through brown in spring, stops to gaze at skies, and recalls the expressions and opinions of taxi drivers, waitresses, and landladies. We all know those moments when life seems an undeserved bonus granted us by a mysterious benefactor. We know, too, those mind-numbing moments when life seems utterly insupportable. After dreaming of being better than we are, we slide into the realization that we may very well be much worse than we dare acknowledge. It is then that we crave assurance of the value of our being here on earth at all. If we're lucky, someone or something edges us beyond our fantasies, and we build toward sanity. But Arthur Bremer is not lucky. He is haunted by the foreknowledge of failure, since nothing in his experience has prepared him for any of the roles he longs to play. He is one of the shadows who sidle past us in the streets with sullen, loosely directed defiance. Through his torturous misspellings, half-comprehended bits of political and cultural knowledge, we are plunged into the ignorance and incompetence that stunt millions of young people today as they have stunted people in the past. Moving from birth through haphazard education and training, demeaning jobs, unemployment, and then shut away from the rest of us in welfare hotels, nursing homes, and state institutions, they are the garbage of a society which spends more on cosmetics, entertainment, and anesthetics than it does on developing human potential or caring for those it does not equip to care for themselves.

Arthur Bremer was nourished by the same societal manure that stains us all. We may not plan defiant revenge as he did, but most of us react with similar impotence at the betrayal we sense in those who control our world. As I write this, American bombers are devastating peasant villages thousands of miles away as no place on earth has ever been ravaged before. But I, like hundreds of millions of my contemporaries, shut off the news, turn to a martini or a football game or whatever diversion will neutralize the impulse to take action against what we protest being done in our name. Because we succeed in submerging our rage, we are defined as sane. At least for the moment. A playwright friend of mine was recently arrested on an airplane for threatening to kill President Nixon. Interviewed by reporters, and thus achieving more attention than his plays have ever brought him, he claimed not to understand what he was doing in a jail cell. He probably didn't intend to kill the President; he may have merely been expressing the hope that someone else would. He is the author of a very successful film in which an advertising executive and a construction worker gun down a roomful of hippies. Unlike Bremer, my friend is not illiterate, nor is he the product of indifference and neglect. He is a Harvard graduate, and before he turned to the hazards of free-lance writing, was a well-paid advertising executive himself. His predicament is a response to the barrage of indigestible fragments of culture and information that pushes us, minute by minute, further from reality. The man who writes the slogans is as victimized as the one who hears them.

We can be entertained in our own homes only by accepting the shrill huckstering of products no one really requires. Knowing we are being cheated and lied to on all levels (from Pentagon

11

reports to claims for the efficacy of detergents), we retreat into a simmering rage which seldom finds a focus. Between commercials, we follow glossy suspense stories created to keep us from switching channels, and forebodings of disaster become second nature to us. Away from the television set, we board a plane fully expecting to be hijacked, and we walk familiar streets choking back irrational fears at the sound of footsteps behind us. But we are Americans and by definition expected to defend our rights, and so we reach for whatever weapon is available. And weapons, even more than irony, abound. Plentiful as they are, they are useless in the hands of the incompetent or the foolhardy, and failure in what we watch so easily accomplished by the heroes of movies and television drama generates a nagging, never extinguished frustration.

This diary is a document of frustration, and an accusation of failure, both of the individual and of the humanity he belongs to. If everything in our salesman's culture boasts a brand name, what distinguishes the name of Arthur Bremer? Is he expected to exist without a label, inferior to a tube of toothpaste or a can of beer? If society will not provide him with his brand name, then he will select one himself and "assassin" has become an unforgettable label in recent years. He chooses the role he will play regardless of his qualifications for it. He's shrewd enough to perceive that others, no more qualified than he, have achieved distinction. They have proof that they exist. Bremer will prove, too, that he was here, locked in paragraphs of history with Nixon, as Oswald is with one

Kennedy brother and Sirhan is with another. The role one chooses to play can replace one's actual role. And what is the actuality for this twenty-one-year-old self-admitted virgin who wistfully writes that even the weeds in the city are taller than his five feet six inches? Bent on attaining lasting fame, Bremer dwells with narcissistic detail upon his inadequacies, deriding them with the contempt usually reserved for others.

He senses his deficiency in the "charisma" that has replaced old-fashioned virtue and tries to achieve momentary attention by having a limousine drive him to downtown Manhattan. Gratified by being "stared at by the poor people," he easily separates himself from them in spite of the evidence that he belongs outside with them staring into the plush interior of the hired car. Later he takes a taxi to the Waldorf-Astoria and "never got looked at by ANYONE." Attention, as Willy Loman's wife said so eloquently, must be paid, and most of us go to some lengths to assure that attention is given us. To Bremer, it is most important that we are dressed for the part we choose to play. Seeing what he believes is the President's limousine parked outside the Embassy in Ottawa, he rushes back to his hotel room, brushes his teeth, takes two aspirin, and changes his suit before hurrying back to get "Nixy-boy." He explains that he wanted "to shock the shit out of the SS men with my calmness." Like an untrained actor, he is more concerned with how he looks than with what he is doing. Enraged because he has missed his opportunity, he compares himself with his notorious predecessor in the role: "Does

13

the world remember if Sirhan's tie was on straight? SHIT, I was stupid!!" But he swears to "give very little if ANY thought to these things on any future attempts."

Often as he rehearses his role, he is never secure in the part. Like many young people, he wants to be something without becoming it. He prepares for his self-assigned leap to fame as carelessly as he spells the words of his native language. Leaving the plane which has just landed in New York City, his name is called over the loudspeaker (which so pleases him that he calls it to the attention of the man sharing the facilities with him) and he is handed the presumably concealed guns he was about to leave behind. In a motel room, waiting to cross the border into Canada, he accidentally discharges his Browning automatic, then cowers in anticipation of his landlady's investigating the shot. Remembering how movie gunmen camouflage the sound of gunshots, he turns on the television set, fortuitously tuning in on machine-gun bursts in a war film of the nineteen-forties. The landlady never appears, and he quite rightly assumes that others are as incompetent as himself. Later, trying to secrete his 9 mm. to get it past the customs, he pushes it beyond retrieval into the inner structure of the car he's driving into Canada. But it doesn't matter: the customs officers don't bother to inspect his car or his luggage upon his entry. They earn, as do all the officials, his contempt: "I instantly lost all respect for the Big Bad Canadian Customs." He is learning that real life lacks the hypoed suspense of *The Man from U.N.C.L.E.* Whatever excitement exists, off screen, at least, must be created by the actor himself. It is much harder to get attention than it seems, and early in his odyssey, Bremer senses that his famous death will evade him, but he doggedly hangs on to hopes of it because he has nothing else.

Unable to follow directions given by garage attendants, and apparently incapable of reading road maps, Bremer gets lost for several hours outside Ottawa, as he drives to kill the President. He reaches Ottawa as Nixon is arriving in his official plane. By now, Bremer has become the part he's playing: casing the airport, he wonders "Would the assassin get a good view," leaving obscure Arthur Bremer behind for the figure who will be in the headlines the next day. He expresses no animosity toward President Nixon, who is merely the vehicle through which Arthur Bremer will achieve stardom. When a news cameraman focuses his lenses upon noisy peace demonstrators, Bremer is insulted that the star of the drama is being neglected for the extras. He is convinced that the act he is prepared to perform will rank in importance with "the start of W[orld] W[ar] I" and that the page in his diary describing it will be "one of the most closely read pages since the Scrolls in those caves." Single-mindedly concentrating on the personal fame the assassination will bring him, he seems not even aware of political consequences nor does he reveal political motivation. His casual explanations of why he risks his own life are contradictory, sometimes within the same sentence: "One of my reasons for this action is money and you the American . . . public will pay me. The silent majority will be my benifactor in the biggest hijack ever!" Such phrases, heard with numbing repetition as the evening news informs us of bombings, earthquakes, police corruption, and airplane thefts, blend into homogenized sound without meaning. Placed within that blender will be Arthur Bremer's name if he succeeds in what he has chosen to play.

As he assumes his role, he evolves an almost intimate relationship with the man he hopes to kill. His references shift from "The President" to "he" to "Nixon" to "Nixy," and, finally, as the grotesque coupling he intends approaches, to "Nixy-boy." Aware that his words will be read long after he's dead, he includes appropriate phrases in the manuscript warning against infringement of copyright. To anyone who dreams of being a published writer, these aspirations to literary status echo that persistent dream of the author: My name will live long after I am no more. Here, it is a heartbreaking plea from one who seems to have entered the world unnoticed but struggles against leaving it unremembered.

Arthur Bremer is aware of these elements in his nature. Having awakened from dreams of glory before, he sometimes derides this most grandiose one, pondering at one point whether he should abandon it completely and go to Hollywood to make his fortune on "the old sivler screen." It is Hollywood, of a previous era, gleaned second-hand through midnight showings on television, that furnishes him with images of himself and others. Suspecting he is being followed by Secret Service agents, he transforms them into Keystone Cops and himself into Charlie Chaplin, a little every-man pitted against authority. He identifies a peace demonstrator in Ottawa as the type "Hollywood hires to play the wagon train attacking Indian." The strongest criticism he expresses is not directed at politicians whose public decisions affect his immediate life, but at popular entertainers. Appalled that Diana Ross watered down her talents for rich whites, he never mentions the hypocrisy shrouding our barbarity in Vietnam or the dismissal of essential human needs for political expediency. He envies Nixon's social life: "one party after another for 4 years," but is much more critical of the flaky apple pie served in a Canadian restaurant. At twenty-one, he knows that life is a sham and a cheat. What little he writes of political information has been garnered from the same source as his entertainment and is reproduced as parroted slogans about American imperialism, the establishment, and the new rebel: "To be a rebel today you have to keep a job, wear a suit & stay apolitical. Now THAT'S REBELLION!"

Where do young men such as this learn what they believe? Where do these words, so muddy in meaning and so resonant in echo, come from? Here we leave Arthur Bremer and turn upon ourselves, passively accepting casual chatter for thought in nightly news broadcasts, convenience for conviction in politics and public morality, and entertainment for reality in most of our waking leisure hours. We brush our teeth in the morning to the sound of celebrities being interviewed, and we drift to sleep at night after sharing their reflections and jokes with Johnny Carson. In the hours between, the Bremers, Sirhans, and Oswalds take us up and down in elevators, wash our dishes, collect our garbage, and patrol our streets. No wonder they eye the rest of us with distrust and envy. Their leaders are no better, if not worse, than they are: Elected officials are openly accused, and occasionally convicted, of bribery, perjury, and flouting the law they vowed to uphold; judges are paid off, gangsters hook kids on heroin in schoolyards, and the corrupt fortunates ride shiny Lincoln Continentals through rubbish-strewn streets, eat $100-a-plate dinners at the Waldorf while migrant children bloat from malnutrition. Values preached in church and taught, if not demonstrated, in schools are nothing but masks rigidly clamped in place to keep the lucky lucky and the others where they belong. Lucky means rich and famous. Secure in affluence and celebrity, symphony conductors, best-selling novelists, and Broadway stars meet before television cameras while the unlucky watch, mixing envy with vengefulness. On the small screens in our living rooms and on the large ones at the drive-ins, even the stupidest among us learn early that crime and sexual promiscuity are rewarded more than what our preachers and teachers advise as a way of life. How can those traditional guardians of morality and culture serve as models today on the perilous journey each human being must make?

Arthur Bremer apparently made that journey by himself. There is no mention here of parents, teachers, friends, or models. The only personal reference is a single line about a girl from whom he had broken off, but "it wasn't about sex." Isolated from others, he occupies himself with day-dreams to avoid coping with the life that races through his flesh. Eventually, it burst through these pages as raw and ribald as thwarted life always is: "the 1st person I held a conversation with in 3 months was a near naked girl rubbing my erect penis & she wouldn't let me put it thru her." In spite of the blatant stimulation to sexual intercourse which permeates all advertising and entertainment today, Arthur Bremer is still a virgin. His attempts to remedy his condition are aided by the most up-to-date marketing and production procedures. He checks the ratings of Manhattan's massage parlors in *Screw,* a newspaper which exploits the hungers of the thwarted and the unwanted, then circles the building warily before finally entering it to be assigned with Alga for "a ½ [hour] session in studio 2" as if they were a singing duo. There, Alga, innocuously doing her job, refuses to let him touch her private parts because it's against the rules, but tries unsuccessfully to bring him to ejaculation. Later, Bremer writes: "Thought I'm still a virgin, I'm thankful to Alga for giving me a peek at what it's like." Locked in common victimization rather than in sexual congress, the naked boy and the bikini-clad girl are partners in a prepackaged encounter. Nothing happens between them that Bremer could not have accomplished more effectively by himself. They are two automatons locked in a grisly charade which denies their humanity as it denies his orgasm. A consumer searching for the most highly advertised pleasure in life is mocked by the mechanics of the marketplace. Yet, only dimly aware that his essential nature has been degraded, Bremer complains merely that the girl accepted a thirty-dollar tip but gave him nothing in return. Upon reflection, he regards her with the fondness one victim feels for another.

The long section on his experience in the massage parlor occurs early in the diary, and may seem extraneous on the surface. But it is actually the most revealing clue to the man himself. It allows us, at the start, to see the boy eager for the most outrageous excesses of sexual abandon, made familiar to him by reading, gossip, and fervid imagination. We never really lose sight of that boy as Bremer starts his passage toward death. His nudity upon the massage table previews his end upon the embalmer's slab, stripped of his pitiful defenses and of the clothes he carefully chose to disguise himself as a "straight" kid no one would ever suspect of planning to kill the President. Only with Alga does his nagging need for celebrity subside. His failure to achieve what all young men long for colors our response to later pages. We smile in appreciation of his boyish pleasure at the sight of the "pure green grass not cut yet from winter" on his arrival in Washington. We recognize the desperate aches and pains through which his body attempts to signal him against what his mind is planning. In a poem attempting to define his motives for the intended assassination, he says his penis made him do it. He may be right. The gun, as popular novelists have taught even the most dim-witted, replaces the natural organ when the latter falls into disuse. After his failure in the massage parlor, Bremer moves steadily toward his victim with the tenderness reserved for the lover.

There is no mention of love in this diary, as if it is an unfamiliar element in his life. He suspects that people dislike him; he claims a girl in a hotel hates him because he left his toenails on the rug at the foot of the bed. Early in the diary, he writes that he "must of begun to cry 8 distint times yesterday night." Cry for what? Or for whom? He will not lift the shield behind which he hides his deepest feelings. He stresses not what he has lost, or never had, but what he will gain. Yet he recognizes the nature of what he plans: "It won't be a nice composed vested suited man—it will be a mad man who kills nixon & he will kill him he will be dead." Such childlike rhythms and repetitions of words are accompanied sometimes on the same page by such pretentious references as "Call me Ismal." Has he really read *Moby Dick* or did he see the movie, or has he merely heard of the prophetic opening words of that classic novel of self-destruction? And does he know the correct spelling of the name but is incapable of remembering it or writing it? More than the irony abounding in these pages is a cultural disorientation, which leads to posing in various roles, culminating in his declaration that "I Am A Hamlet."

The murderer in literature, from *Oedipus* to *Hamlet* to Camus' *The Stranger,* is the mirror none of us can resist gazing into. Novelists are rarely murderers except in their imaginations. Here, we come face to face with a Raskolnikov but without the guidance of a Dostoevski, who wrote to his publisher that his hero "had submitted to certain,

21

strange incomplete ideas that float on the wind."
A hundred years after the publication of *Crime and Punishment,* ideas are flung over the airwaves every minute. It should surprise no one that the classic justifications of murder—revenge, passion, ambition, self-preservation—do not apply to Arthur Bremer. Like Camus' Meursault, he is indifferent to justification: "Ask me why I did it & I'd say 'I don't know', or 'Nothing else to do', or 'Why not?' or 'I have to kill somebody'." He is the existentialist assassin—unprepared, incompetent, self-mocking, certain only of the news value of his act: "It may sound exciting & fascinating to readers 100 years from now—as the Booth conspricy seems to us today." But he cannot share the stage with other conspirators. He is willing to co-star only with a super-star. Thwarted in his attempts to shoot the President, he indulges in alternate fantasies: "To wear white tie & tails & get Nixon-boy, WOW! If I killed him while wearing a sweatty tee-shirt some of the fun & Glamore would defionently be worn off." Immersed in the habitual preoccupation of the star with his appearance, Bremer is late for his entrance and fails again, but he consoles himself with another fantasy: "I even thought of killing as many SS men as I could. Because I was pissed at them & myself and Nixon killing 5 or 6 Secret Service agents would get me in the papers SOMETHING to show for my effort. Killing 'em right in front of Nixon—dig it!? . . . Didn't want to get emprisoned or killed in an unsuccessful attempt. To have absolutely nothing to show—I couldn't take that chance."

Unwilling to accept total blame for his failures, Bremer accuses others of foiling him. The peace demonstrators in Ottawa had brought about stronger security than he had anticipated: "to this day" (all of ten days after the fact) "I blame them for partial responsibility in failing my attempt." Bremer follows the President to Washington hoping to get another chance there, but he runs out of funds and decides to return home to Milwaukee. There he reads in the newspaper that the President had been shaking hands with tourists at the same time Bremer had left the city: "I could of killed him for doing that alone."

Giving up all hope that the President will ever be accessible, he looks around for another victim. He considers George McGovern but dismisses that as too minor a production. Upon learning that Wallace is scheduled to make speeches across the lake in Michigan, he settles upon him, admitting he has chosen second-best: "I won't even rate a T.V. enteroption in Russia or Europe when the news breaks—they never heard of Wallace. If something big in Nam flares up I'll end up at the bottom of the 1st page in America. The editors will say—'Wallace dead? Who cares.'" But the actor does not exist without a vehicle, and a second-rate one is better than none. Bremer drives to Michigan, where he gets lost for several hours in the suburbs of Dearborn trying to locate a rally he's heard about on television. He finds it and mingles with the Wallace supporters. Again he identifies with his victim and Governor Wallace becomes "Wally." Watching him closely at the rallies, Bremer sympathizes because the audience

23

is not sufficiently responsive: "I DID THE MOST HAND CLAPPING, ALL THE SHOUTING, & WAS GOING TO START 3 DIFFERENT STANDING OVATIONS BUT FELT THE CROWD WOULDN'T FOLLOW ME. . . . A great disappointment for him I bet. Poor guy. What would he have done without me?"

As he shifts targets and is forced to adapt his role in order to accommodate his new co-star, it becomes clear that this journal is, in effect, a film scenario in which the author/actor projects himself into situations almost banal in their familiarity: unmarked roads harass him, old ladies eye him suspiciously from doorways, good-natured Canadian Mounties advise him to move on, Secret Service men tag his footsteps, and his luggage is secretly tampered with in his hotel room. The camera is riveted on Bremer himself, another hero of a culture which abandons common sense in its glorification of the diseased and the perverted. We have accepted midnight chiselers, drug smugglers, hookers, crime syndicate families, and rural criminal terrorists as heroes of a bloodstained folklore. Why shouldn't Arthur Bremer reach for his place in the pantheon along with Bonnie and Clyde, the midnight cowboys, and the easy riders?

Lacking professional skill with which to sugarcoat the image of himself that will engage our empathy, he is forced to fall back upon raw material: that gnawing sense of failure, bred in the bone and destined to haunt him as long as he lives. But he does engage us, against our will, just as those prototypes of the misbegotten among us do in films and fiction. Since we live in affluence, the losers achieve sainthood. Warily circling the anticipated delights of the massage parlor, Bremer felt like "I was going to get raped." Leaving it as unfulfilled as he'd been upon entering, the baffled postadolescent later writes: "I left without looking back, a mistake, a great mistake in my life time."

He is right. The ecstatic mystery that forms us all in the beginning and warms us in the dark of night might have awakened him to other ways of using himself. But it was closed off to him, through his own timidity and the misrepresentation of products which is now inherent in advertising. He tried to stamp his name upon the consciousness of posterity by hoping to embrace in his life's final convulsion someone whose name would be Bremer's passport to remembrance. After all, John Wilkes Booth is known to more people today than is his once-famous actor-brother. And what more exultant death than to expire on television before the rapt attention of the millions who perceive the reality of the world and the identity of others through its magic? How else can five-feet-six of twenty-one-year-old virgin flesh make its presence known to the indifferent world? After all, it's easy. Anyone can buy a gun and slip over the border with it undetected. Anyone can synchronize his actions to a publicly broadcast schedule of a President or mingle with a candidate's supporters on the village green. Anyone can be famous. For a moment. Until the retaliatory fusillade, or until the prison gates clang behind him as they have behind the pitiful and oddly touching Arthur Bremer.

All human aspiration is touching because it separates us from the other species. But the aspiration for fame is perhaps the most touching because it is the most treacherous. When I was asked to write this introduction, I couldn't remember who Arthur Bremer was. So much has happened since May, 1972, so many names and faces have flashed past our retinas. The world is populated by names we remember only for a week or two, if that. So perhaps Bremer is, as he feared, "just another god Damn failure." If anyone can be a failure at twenty-two. And who decides who is a failure? During recent days of unprecedented bombings in Southeast Asia, I find it hard to believe anyone's life can match the failure of Richard Nixon's. But that's only my opinion. History will record Nixon's name prominently and Arthur Bremer's will be forgotten. His life is not over, as he hoped it would be; it is merely hidden from the society that betrayed him by cheapening the values we all live by and robbing him of meaning beyond what we can glean from these pathetic scribblings about his hopes, his fears, and his need for future renown, aspects of the human being we all share with him as we share the shame that produced him.

HARDING LEMAY

January 1, 1973

AN ASSASSIN'S
DIARY

After I wrote the last page &
showered & ate lunch I feel claimed
down now. Heard a song on the radio
though—was turning away from rock &
roll music which only wore on me &
got a conservative station with a
girl singing "Go ahead & hate your
nabor, go ahead & cheat a friend"—
but I heard, at the time, Go ahead &
kill (or shoot) your nabor, which
disturbed me greatly.

APRIL 4, 1972 TUSDAY 6:30 a.m.

Hurray! Hurray! Great day for
democracy & capitalism! A 50% voter
turn out is expected! Now THAT'S
confidence in America. Tired to bury
pages 1-148 in Sheridan Park just
south of Milw. on the lake front at
8-10 but the place was too crowded.
Kids in parked cars & cars
positioning for a good dark spot.
The ground was too rocky. I was
too near a land fill sight (I'll
never recover it after few weeks)
& a big 600 foot sheer cliff! Want
to get rid of it in or near the big
city.
Oh Jesus! My birth was at 2:40 p.m.
August 21, 1950 and that's the time

29

my plane leaves. Ashes to Ashes.
Copy of any birth certificate cost 2
bucks.

APRIL 5, 1972

Consider yesterday, the last
minute rush, the burying of the book
& the trip & NO CAR one of my worst
days in years. If I attempted to say
half of what was done to me, I
wouldn't do the emotion of despair
justice. You heard of "<u>One Day in
the Life of Ivan Dynisovich</u>"?
Yesterday was my day. I could write
150 pages alone describing that day.

Wallace got his big votes from
Republicans who didn't have any
choice of candidates on their own
ballot. Had only about $1055 when I
left.

Took a 4 hour walk around this
slum. Alleys and some parts of
sidewalks are dirt. Not concrete
dirt covered, but dirt. Some of the
weeds between the curbs & the
sidewalks are taller than me 5'6.
But mostly they average between my
waist & chest level, some times
growing this high on both sides of
the sidewalk giving an impression
of walking thru an animal trail in
a woods. Litter abounds. A junk
dealer with a truck to pick up from

the vacant lots & streets has his
fortune made. Cars are often parked
very near or on the pedestrian walks
between city blocks, some with a
tire or two removed & other
deformities. These junk cars are
parked on the city streets. The
natives have been seen parking cars
with the engine running & going
across the street to shop. In mid
morning & mid afternoon were
observed school aged children some
with parents. Perhaps Easter
vacation. My Howard Johnson's is $23
and $1 occupation tax & some other
tax. I'm charged 20¢ per call from
my room which is very noticably
smaller than my Madison, Wis. room
for under $17 total. I'm at 140 st.
and 135 av. (it may be the other way
around). Down town is barely visable
with binocculars, being a good 12
miles off on the horizon. I'll spend
tomorrow there & get out of this
cold peopled place.

Could buy a car for around $400—
may do it. Live at YMCA. Have
one in Canada?

Read the sexy parts of the Little
Red Book. (furnished with the room)
Whores & cleansing & circumcision
& incest. Must of been hot stuff
2,000 years ago. I'll pick up the
modern version tomorrow.

Got a little tanning from the clear skys. Must of begun to cry 8 distint times yesterday night. Watched T.V. 'till 2:30 a.m. Great movies of the '40's. Surprisingly got up at 8:00.

Damn this Avis and in my luck.

And the credit card application.

S H I T ! I've got a thousand bucks. If I can't get a car (auto lincese into Canada?) & live for 10 days on that. W E L L !
And if I fail _____

_____

_____

I give a puzzeled disbelieving look to the New Yorkers accent. A curious distortion of the language.

Yesterday I had one wash cloth and 2 bath towels, today the opposite. The girl doesn't like me because I left my toe nails on the rug at the foot of my bed.

Should of taken the fucking Airport Helicoptor to downtown. I'm so close . . . so close.

APRIL 13, 1972

A life time of events has happened since I last wrote in here. I didn't write because I was tired of it bored with it. I wanted to ACT instead. And I didn't want to confess in here after I went thru so much to bury the first 150 or so pages. Let me TRY to sum things up BRIEFLY. I sure wish I had written 1500 words a day & had it befor me now for entertainment.

My last night at the Howard Johnson's in the Jamaica area, New York City I didn't sleep much. A beautiful naked lady across a parking lot in the next motel out by her window (floor to ceiling) smoking cigarettes & I had to watch her. Her table room light was on & a thin vail of curtain allowed me

to watch as she passionately kissed
a man who wore cloths. I never saw
them in each others arms more than
a minute at a time. They must of
been fighting. Thru binocculars I
saw them gesture like Italians &
open their mouths very wide often.

For $16 I took a helicoptor to
Wall St., closer to Le Guardia. Some
guy asked me what I thought of
helicoptors & the possible
improvements that could be made upon
them. I guess he designed 'em.
Couldn't help him. Got a limousine
(Lincoln Continnetal [Nixon was in
one today]) for $11 (an hour) ($2
tip) & the chaffuer in chaffuer's
hat (was hack driver for a long
time, but not in last 7 years) gave
me a tour thru the open markets &
Chinatown & the Bowery & narrow
streeted financial district. I asked
him for help in getting me a hotel
(a lot of 'em are residential only)
& he got me the Fifth Ave. Hotel.
Sounds impressive but it didn't
compare to the Howard Johnson's.
Kids running in the halls (in
diapers) a stink in the hall and
room, a dump. Nice looking
restaurant from the outside but it
wasn't open 'till 11:30 the next
morning. I ate at a hero sandwitch
joint, got sick on the shit.

Walked 20 miles (10 blocks to a
mile) thru mid-Manhattan. Never saw
so many street venders. On a few
streets were signs "This street
patroled by----private police."
WOW! I always carried my gun outside
my hotel in N.Y.C. I really felt
good being stared at by the poor
people in my limosine. Took a taxi
to the Waldorf-Astoria & never got
looked at by ANYONE. Driver bobed
his head a lot, a nervos wreck. I
thought the Waldorf was the best
N.Y.C. had to offer. I was wrong.
For $37 plus I got a room little
better than the $23 Fifth Ave.
joint. The bed cryed-out every time
I turned & at night I could hear the
beds in the 2 rooms next to mind do
the same. I took a lot of their
stationary that's what I payed for.
They spend all their money on their
lobby, & hallways to a lesser
degree. The individual rooms are
flops. Maybe the $60-$180 suites are
something. Rooms are $23-$40. And
I had twin beds in my room! Park Av.
traffic was S H I T T Y . Horns
honked Friday night 'till 2:30 a.m.,
kept me awake 'till 4:00.
    No one under 25 can rent-a-car in
N.Y. state. I made a 8 am
reservation home. --left too late.
But WAIT . . .

After 3 days in N.Y. I decided to
go to a massage parlor
at 11 pm I looked up their ratings
in Screw newspaper, checked the ones
I wanted and was going to 3 or 4
that night. I couldn't do it. I
walked past a place & then got lost.
(on purpose maybe). I felt like I
was going to get raped. Called the
best place for a reservation & was
told "You just come in, sir." I
twisted my guts for hours sitting
before the phone with fear and
anticipation & then was told that.
I put the phone right down cussed
them & went straight to bed for an
anticipated 3 hours before my
flight. Overslept. Made a 4 pm
reservation. Was kind of glad I
still had time to go to a model
studio. It was 3 blocks from the
Waldorf, the Victorian. I walked
past it about 6 times then ate
lunch at a self-service, then
walked past it AT LEAST 12 more
times. I had to think things thru
and get relaxed & this & that
& the other. Walked into an Adult
book store to try to get a horny
feeling. Lousy boring fuck books
& the good photo magazines were
wrapped up in cellophane. Fuck
them. Walked past it & down the
block & around the block and

stopped at a street corner a hell
of a lot of times. Tryed to see a
25¢ dirty movie but they were
closed, it was Sunday. Had justed
watched that morning & made fun of
a dopey preacher on T.V. & figured
if he was against it I wanted it.
Watched young female asses bounce
for encouragement, wasn't a hell of
a lot of 'em. When you want a
girl . . . never around.

APRIL 19, 1972

Guess I was too bored with
writting to even finish my last
entry. I think I remember I was
tired and wanted to sleep, finish
up the summary the next day. I'll
try to finish it now. I have to turn
back to see how far I got.
Saw a hairy hippie type leave
the entrance to the Victorian. Two
old ladys standing & talking right
in front of the place finally leaft
(they were begin to give me funny
looks) & I some how walked up the
screky stairs into the place on
the 2nd floor. It was nicely
furnished, you could see they made
an effort the stairs (carpet
covered) screked, that's all. A
hairy character asked if was there
before & showed me a booklet of

about 20 nude & near nude girls &
said that 2 of them were working
that day, a Sunday afternoon.

I picked out the blonde (the best
looking I thought). The 2 were
sitting on a sofa off to my left.
I was conscience of someone there
but never looked directly in their
direction until the guy said, "Alga
you have a 1/2 session in studio
2."($18) This was right after I
signed a statement that I would
"behave in a gentalmanly manner."
Alga & I looked at each other,
I thought her rear end was
kind of fat & her face & hair
& figure generally attractive.
She led me into a room
locked it, turned the lights out
& lit incest all with her back
generally towards me. Piped in
music began. I handed her 3 tens
& said we'd have to take it easy
as I just ate lunch, she didn't
hear me (I think I was kind of
wispering rather than my voice
cracking) & had to repeat it one
or twice. She glanced at my
offering hand & said "put it on
the table."
    Again with her back toward me
she began to undress. I took off
my vested bussiness suit & overcoat

and layed on my stomach on the
massage table, nude. She didn't
see my organ yet. I started some
talk about a burglar alarm that
was ringing & was ringing for the
last 2 days. We talked about the
weather.

She started by massaging the
fleshy part above and behind
my collar bones, then the upper
back, lower back, buttocks, &
legs. She was compleatly nude
except for a yellow nylon bikini
panty.
   "Do you want to turn over now?"
I obliged and was fully erect &
pretty much relaxed. We had talked
about the music, stero tapes rather
than a radio. I looked at her more
closely now and saw she was
beautiful. Beautiful. Her breasts
were perfectly beautiful her rear
end not fat AT ALL. I glided my
hand over her back & side & rear
for a closer inspection.
   "You're not supposed to do that."
   "What?"
   "Touch me."
   "Why?"
   "That's the rules."
   "Are you kidding?"
   I had gently held & caressed her
waist line with one hand as I lay

down & she did not protest. She saw
I was looking at her private parts.
When I slided my hand down she
started this line of conversation.
I thought she wanted more money
before we started the heavy
stuff. I sat up & looked into
her beautiful big brown eyes.
"Are you kidding?" (that's not a
elugie here it's true)

She talked about "the rules."
Customers aren't allowed to touch
the girls. By this time she was
massaging my erect penis with one
hand. Up & down too quickly to be
enjoyed. I moved her hand in mind
in a slower more pleasurable motion.
We talked about "the rules." Then
there was a long silence as she
continued working on my legs &
I looked at her & thought the whole
thing thru.

I sat up gently & tryed to put
my head to her breasts she stepped
back just out of head resting range.
I kept my hand, which was around
her waist, on her side & we looked
at each other a long time. Later I
slowly reached out to brush her
brest with my hand, I moved slowly
enought for her to move away but
I surely didn't want her to. She
covered with her arm a little. I
sat up again & looked into her eyes.

She looked directly into mine. I
think I recongised that same look in
Joan. (that defience, but it wasn't
about sex we fought over) She wasn't
going to give ground.

I layed back down & started
talking about her tips. She was
open about it. "Sometimes I get $2,
$5, $10, $15, $25, or $30." I had
given her $30., & didn't know,
wasn't sure that she had counted it.
    "Why do you get $30 sometimes."
    "Because the customers like me."
    "Why?" A silence before I said,
"What do you do for $30 that you
don't do for $2?"
    She looked right at me & damn it
cause she said, "Nothing."
    Another short silence. "You said
that one of the rules was that the
customers was supposed to climax
if you can't do it this way (she
was using her hand) then lets' do
it another way."
    "This is the only way I can do
it?"
    "What. Don't you read books?"
    "Sure."
    "What books do you read?"
    "Oh, mostly horoscope books?"
    We both knew I was talking about
sex books. So I changed the subject
a little. Tryed to talk about

something she was interested in.
"I'm Leo. What sign are you?"
"I'm Virgo." Damn, she was still
defensive! She said this with a
very very little smile & nod &
looked at me. Damn.

"You don't like your job do you?"
"Not really."
"Then why are you here?"
"I have another job. I'm only here
on weekends."
"What do you do"
"I'm a telephone operator at an
airlines."

She said she didn't go to school.
I sensed that she did. I never heard
of a phone operator for an airlines.
I had told her I was in N.Y. for 4
days & was leaving in 2 hours by
plane. Thought she wanted to satisfy
my question with a lie. Thought she
didn't like me for my crew cut &
straight cloths. She was dressed
somewhat like a hippie, when she
was dressed.

She was here only for the money &
knew she could make more by fucking
but wouldn't. Whenever she was close
I held her more private parts & she
did not protest. Told her she had a
warm tummy. She wouldn't remove her
bikini, "rules". I slipped my hand
up & darted it near & away from her
breast over & over again, never

42

touching it but getting close &
driving her mad with anticipation.
I stopped & smiled. Guess she was
relieved.

She told me she was 20. I said I
was 21. I know I look older in that
suit (& that spair tire I gained).

I felt sorry for the kid. She was
just like everybody else. It was
a job & she was only in it for the
money. I sat up for the last time.
"I'm sorry." Maybe she didn't
understand. I repeated myself once
or twice & shook her arm gently for
enphisis. She smiled. I said,
"O. K.?" She shook her head. I knew
her better now. She was the quiet
type. She had said that for fun she
went to "wo-gees." "Where everyone
takes off their cloths & makes love
to each other." That in a response
to an earlier question after she
refused my advances. Thought she
was making that up too. She had also
said the boss made up the rules &
that she could get fired for
fucking, though not in those words.
I had said I wouldn't tell. She
said she would because she was very
honest. I went into a crazy
confusion at that. I'm sure she
never layed with anyone on the job.
Any one. But looking back now I
rememmber she was nude & wore a

wide smile in the photo I picked
her out from. Maybe a nude shot was
one of the bosses' "rules" also.
(Lousy amature box camera shots.)

Earlier I had told her she could
push & pull on that thing for a
week & I couldn't come. It was true.
I needed, I wanted & was prepared
for a wild 1/2 hour of sucking &
fucking & tongueing & everything.
Just looking at bare however
beautiful tits & getting a hand
job weren't going to do it.

I commented that she must have
strong fingers. She invited me to
feel her forearms & smiled when I
did. Time was up.

A little buzzer rang & went off
by itself. We had never even begun.

I went to my cloths to dress &
she went to hers. I asked her to
wipe the excess off (of my oily
dick) but she misunderstood & wiped
the excess oil in the heated
container onto it.

She commented about my yellow
underpants being like hers. I
thought how wonderful if my pants
could get to know her pants. But
I just said, "Yeah. These are my
hot pants."

She I refer to her in my thoughts
as "Brown-eyes" waited till we were

44

both fully dressed. I asked her why
she went to wo-gees & she said she
just liked them I said she was a
crazy girl & rubed her pants
covered ass. She opened the door
& I left without looking back, a
mistake, a great mistake in my
life time.

It surprises me that I could
rememmber everything we said April
the 8th & today is the 19th.
Thought I'm still a virgin, I'm
thankful to Alga for giving me a
peek at what its like.
But earlier I was angry. I felt
I had payed her to give _her_ a good
time. She goto feel me everywhere
but _everywhere._ And I couldn't even
see hers! And it had cost me $48.
She got $30 plus for 1/2 an hour.
Working two jobs, I didn't gross
that much a day. I stood close to
her after it thinking that a horny
man hates nothing as much as he
hates a cock-teaser & that she would
be a thief not to return a part of
(or all of) the $30. (The $30 men
"like" her & I didn't "like" her.
I was more like a $2 man.) But she
kept it & complaimented me on my
suit. I told her it was lousy.
(Just a disguise to get close to

45

Nixon. I wouldn't wear a ugly thing
& spend $70 plus for it for any
other reason).

All my nervousness was for
nothing. I spent almost all the
time attacking her & she politely
defended herself. Once she sniffled
& I asked if she was crying. "Of
course not. What do I have to cry
about?"

I went straight to the Astoria &
took a cab to the Westside Airlines
Terminal on 42nd Street. A young
black driver with a funny first
name that all black mothers seem to
give their kids. He stopped & sped
up stopped & sped up & I asked him
to quit it befor I puke all over
his cab. We talked about the
careless drivers & dangerous traffic
& he said 3 separate times, "This
is New York, man," & shook his
head. Arrived with a reseration
but without a ticket 15 minutes
before my plane was scheualed to
leave, about 4:00 p.m. United had
the biggest counter at Le Guardia
& the most people waiting in lines
in front of it. I got to the
counter 10 minutes after scheuled
departure. The guy couldn't hold
it for me.

I think he said United had no
other flights to Milwaukee until
Monday afternoon. He directed me
way across the building to the
Northwest counter. It was the
week-end & the whole damn airport
was busy. He had a 5:00 (I think)
flight to Milwaukee all full up.
But I got a stand-by ticket on it.
If a reservation didn't show up to
buy his ticket, I got the flight. I
carryed my bags, he didn't want me

to check them yet, to a seat &
paced all around the seating area.
I needed a car to hide the guns in
to get across the border with them.
I felt that alone in my baggage or
on my body they would be found out
right away. And I had to meet Nixon
in Ottawa by the 13th (his arrival).
Thursday the 13th. I was lucky to
get a seat at the boarding gate it
was so full. This plane came from
somewhere, went to N.Y., then Milw.,
then Minneapolis, St. Paul. Thats
why so many people.

I GOT A SEAT, seat C (of A, B, C)
in row 33 (of 33 rows in the plane).
Whereas befor in a sparsly populated
plane in the 3rd row from the front
(1st class) I had a smooth trip &
excellent service, this trip was
lousy. A fat boring sheltered snob
of a therolgy student talked
non-stop with a equally sheltered
& fasinated (always smiling) high
school student. I waited 30 minutes
for dinner & when I got it, last in
the whole plane, we had turbilence
& the "fasten seat belts" sign went
on. Impossible to do with the dinner

table down. I hurryed & drank down
half my coffee befor it spilled over
my pants. Got away with only a tie
stain and an everlasting preduice
against theology students & capacity
plane trips.

I could hear & watch the
stuardesses privately talk & work
way back their. It's a job their in
it for what they can get. One of
'em wispered "shit" a couple times.

Wonder how much money there is in
theology.

APRIL 21, 1972 FRIDAY

The funnyest thing happened to
me when I arrived in N.Y. just after
I got off the plane. I forgot my
guns! I was in a washroom when I
heard my name over the loud speaker.
WOW! The captain of the plane smiled
& nodded as he gave me them. In
the wash room, I didn't quiet hear
the announcment & asked a fella
next to me if he heard what was
said. He didn't. "Well they
mentioned my name." I thought a
couple seconds & said, "Oh yeah,
now I know!" Irony abounds.

In Milwaukee at Mitchell Field, I got dissy watching every one's luggage go round & round for 15 minutes or more (probaly more) untill I finally got mine. I waited for a cab outside, then got smart & walked in front of the other cab-waiters to where the cabs first enter the terminal area. Got the first one that came along. Even so, the cabbie had me share it with 2 guys traveling together.

That night was frantic. I did everything very quickly because I figured I was behind scheule. I could of, should of been in Ottawa by then if I was 25 & had a credit card. In the old German war movies the Nazies always asked everyone for "your papers". Today the motels & rent-a car firms want "your credit card".

I did my cloths first thing because that would take the most time. 2 loads one light, one dark, just what I had in my bags.

I look at my map. I wanted to enter Canada in a relatively out of the way area. Too long and time

consuming around the Great Lakes
thru Minnesota. I choose just north
of Detroit. I called the Chesapeke
& Ohio Car Ferry (across Lake
Michigan to Ladington, Michigan &
they had a boat leaving about 2:30
that night, about 2 hours away. I
decided to take it rather then drive
around the Lake thru Illinois. I
figured I could catch some sleep
that night & be moving at the same
time.

When I leaft for N.Y. City I knew
I had a front right flat tire on
my car. It was a Sun night & I
really had to look for a station.

Went to a place which had charged
my dead battery once. Pulled off to
the side of the sevice area. The
place gave a free car wash (inside)
to any one buying any amount of gas
that night. Some fucking thing I
never heard of before not just a
fill ANY amount.

The guy said sure he could fix
the flat but I'd have to wait for
the wash jobs ahead of me.

I had another guy check my oil in
the mean time. I checked the water
& left the hood up for him. He put
in a can of 10-40. I was still
waiting around & at that time I
thought I would drive to Canada that
night. I paged thru the Sunday
Journal for News of Nixon's trip.
Nothing there. I asked each station
attendent if he heard anything about
Nixon going to Canada. No, they
were to busy to read a paper or
watch the news. They must of smelled
too much gasoline & it ruined their
brains. I pulled up to the pump to
get a fill up befor going into the
enclosed area to get the tire
patched. Then one of the guys
motioned me forward into the service
stall. I figured I could get a fill
later on & pulled up just in front
of the doors. Then a 1/2 minute
wait. Conversation inside between
the guys.

"Can you pull in tomorrow?"
"I'LL PULL RIGHT OUT THIS FUCKING
STATION!"

They wanted to close for the
night. I backed up & flip-floped
around the block remmembering just
then that I didn't pay for the oil.

I pulled into a smaller station
(one I deliberatly passed up on my
way to the first) & the guy said he
didn't have the jack he needed. I
told him I'd move my car in 2
minutes & ran 2 blocks to the 1st
station to pay for the oil. Ran
back & drove off to the place the
jack-less guy recomended.

A high school kid & his girl were
there talking quietly. Kid seemed
disturbed that someone would pull
into his station, a big name place
like the first, and disturbe his
romance. He didn't have the patches!

"If a service station doesn't have
the patches who does?"

"I don't know".

"Maybe I should try a negligy
store".

He walked back to his girl in
silence.

I drove across the 16th St.
Viaduct. The big Car Care Center was
closed. Compleatly closed down. I

drove further up the street & found
a dingy place, the only place open.
It was about 10 o'clock. The hole
was to big to be patched & I had
put an even larger one in the tire
by driving on the flat. He changed
tires for about $3, I don't really
remember. His fat ugly girl friend
made jokes about my car antenna,
dents, etc. as she fed her face with
a soda. I drove across the street
for a gas fill at a penny less per
gallon than that place.

It sure felt real good to be
riding tall in the saddle again!
But I did notice a dent in the
wheel. The tire wobbled back &
forth when I shook it. I cost
about $22 to get across the lake.
The ship's clerk struck up a
conversation with me & we talked
about travel. He let me have a
room at the day rate (about $5)
rather than charge me the night
rate (about double). Good man! I
wanted to get some sleep that night
because I felt sure I would be
driving all the next day. The people
laying on the sofas in the longe
looked liked uncomfortable dogs.

It took 6 hours to cross the Lake. I was in bed & we were moving before I knew it. Had a very comfortable ride & a good sleep, about 5 hours. I had a surprishing amount of energy on that short a sleep the next morning. The big ship had only about a dozen passengers that night. But lots of fright cars down below.

Call me Ismal.

Drove along Highway 10 thru beautiful green Central Michigan. Drove from about 9:am to 3:pm I guess. Worryed that my wobblely front right wheel would come right off but it settled in somewhat & gave no real trouble. Stopped & spent the night in Port Huron, Michigan & that was an adventure too.

I still hadn't hidden or even found a place to hide my guns in the car. I envisioned a hell of a good serch at the border. And I had forgotten my car registration. Ask around & called the U.S. Customs about it. I had read that I needed proof of auto ownership before I could take a car into Canada.

I even planned to fly back to
Milwaukee just to get it & come
right back. The town had no
direct service to Milwaukee,
I would of had to drive down
to Detroit. I even envisioned
chartering a plane to take me back
to Milwaukee direct & take off
within 2 hours with the car
registration in my pocket. I didn't
want to waste more time.

I filled my guns with all the
bullets they would hold 14 in the
Browning, 5 in the Charter Arms .38.
That night I thought of where I
could possible hide the guns.

Picking up the Browning 9mm I
accidently fired off a shot! I
squeezed the trigger on purpose but
I forgot that I had loaded it just
hours before. My entire head rang
from the powerful blast. In the
room my ears felt the blast vibrate
off the walls & return. I felt sure
the woman who rented me the room
would come running & pound on my
door to see if I had killed my self
with that one loud bang or what.

I turned the T.V. on. In the movies
they always turn the T.V. or radio
on & way up to muffle gun shots.
I gave it a real life test, only
AFTER THE SHOT WAS FIRED. I thought
I'd be hauled off to jail for
carrying a gun at the least. I
rehearsed a speech to the lady. "I
accidently fired my gun". What the
fuck else could I say? Would she
believe anything else? I found a
war movie on & if I wasn't fucking
lucky the Americans were giving the
Japs every thing they had. I turned
the sound WAY up to pretend to be
an inconsiterate nabor to the rooms
next to me. (The small Howard
Johnson's lobby & my room shared a
common wall, I wasn't sure if the
room next to me on the other side
of my room was occupided but knew
the one next to it was.) A lot of
Japs must of been slautered but
none of the T.V. shots bounced off
the walls like mind did.

I thought maybe the lady didn't
rush into my room right away
because she was calling the
police to investigate it for her.
"There's a man with a gun in here,
officer!" 15 minutes passed.
I knew cops were slow to come
when you wanted them. I put the
gun out of sight but somewhere
where I could surrender them right
away if asked to. I didn't want it
to look like I had hid them. I
put 'em in seperate places, prepared
to give up the Browning on a
Carrying Concealed Weapons charge
& still have the .38 for bussiness.
(The lady knew I was going into
Canada. The cops would ask why I
was taking a gun across the border.
All this & more going thru my
mind . . .). after 25 minutes I sat
back & started enjoying the movie.
Nothing happened.

It took a while but I found the
path of the bullet. Luck I didn't
shoot a finger off or something. I
was sitting on the big bed & the
bullet went thru a smaller bed
into the floor I guess. No basement
in the building I reasoned.

Thru a blanket, 2 sheets & a
matress I followed a small clean
hole. I couldn't find where it came
out but there was a large tear in
the cloth under the bed. Maybe I
caused it. I thought the bullet
struck a wooden support in the bed
& stayed there. Examining the
carpet, I found a small barely
noticable (& hidden by the small bed
& the curtains in front of the floor
to ceiling window) white (wood?)
hole in the carpet. Looking closely
& probing with my pen knife I could
not find the bullet, a piece of
evidence I wanted. Still don't know
for sure weather the bullet is in
the bed or that hole in the carpet.

If I had held the gun a few inches
higher or had been standing up,
I'm positive I would of broken the
large window. The bullet would of
traveled on who knows where (my
car was a few feet right of the
bedroom in front of my door).

THEN there would of been trouble.

The night befor this I had
disposed of all my excess
ammunition, cartiage boxes (2)
& a booklet explaining the operation
of the Browning.

I carefully tore the booklet up
& likewise the boxes. I drove thru
the quiet residential areas (the
small town had poor street lighting
compared to Milwaukee & ALL the
alleys in Milwaukee are lit up
at night). All the bullets went
into one sewer. The torn box
went into another & the other box
into still another. I let the torn
bits of the booklet go to the
winds every few blocks. Found
an extra bullet in a pocket & thru
it into a field. Thru the 2 gun
cases into a poond in a vacant lot.
They floated damn it but it was the
best I could do & I wasn't about to
go on in after them. Thru them
away in day light just befor I
crossed the border.

I picked up the mat in my car
trunk & found a snuke little hole
that the .38 fit perfectly. The
9mm, half cocked & safty on I put
in a corridor in the trunk over

the right rear wheel. It was
visable when looked at closely. The
morning of the border crossing I
took my long armed ice scraper &
pushed the gun farther in as far
as I could.

A mistake. It fell forward and
down in front of the rear wheel
never to be recovered. At the time
I thought maybe I had push it a
little too far.

I wanted to wash the filthy car
befor border inspection. To look
more respectable and innocent.
But I thought an automatic car wash
would rust my .38, exposed to the
elements by a hole in the bottom
of the car. (Both the hole I put it
into & the one below it were made
by the factory. I found a wealth of
hiding places built into my '67
Rambler Rebel. I used the ones I
choose most likely to be overlooked)
I found a self-wash 100 yeards from
my room across a parking lot.
Confussed, I rinse the car clean
& never switched on the "detergent
wash" button. Except for the dents,

it did look respectable. I had also
dusted the inside.

I knew dogs were trained to smell
gun powder & hoped that the heavy
smell of gasoline & <u>HEET</u> gasoline
additive in my trunk would ward off
the nice doggies from my cargo.

After unloading the gun cases &
dripping dry from the car-wash, I
went to the border. I turned the
radio to a conservative station to
relax me & show the nice border
guard I wasn't a hippie. With my
short hair cut, I worryed that he
might take me for a Army deserter.
Clean shaven, I had taken my beard
off the night before, relaxed &
confident with all the proables &
possablities in the back of my mind,
I slowed down to be inspected.

Canada had crooked teeth and a
moustach. He asked where I was
from, where I wanted to go, for how
long & if I had anything to declair.

(I was prepared for this last
question, I was going to say, "I
declair its a nice day." But I just
asked, "What should I declair?")

"Anything you might leave in
Canada? Do you have any
merchandise?"

I looked around & said I had a
type recorder. Nothing I would leave
or sell in the country. Thought
thoughts of a few hundred bucks &
a few bullets raced thru my head.
He said,"O.K." That was the great
border inspection. He never looked
thru my baggage I never left my car.
I instantly lost all respect for the
Big Bad Canadian Customs.

I asked Canada if I could exchange
my American funds for Canadian
currency. He told me where to go.
I pulled on to the wrong place &
a guy in the same uniform as Canada
asked if I was sent to undergo duty
inspection (pay an entry tax on
merchandise I guess). I stayed cool

& told him I just wanted to exchange money, a dume lost tourist from America. I had almost $700. Old Mrs. Canada at the exchange booth took 1% off of that. Maybe as a service charge (I doute it) or as the par rate of exchange (more likely).

Driving on I thought of what an ass hole I was. I could of had enough guns in my baggage & in the trunk to start a revolution in Canada. Two artilery pieces & a 1,000 machine guns & a million rounds of ammo & 12 pigmyes to carry it all on their heads. Enought drugs for every one & his brother. I felt stupid for going thru all the trouble & worry I did. I had wanted to get deep inside the country as soon as possible (thoughts of the cops looking for the gun that made that bullet hole haunted me.) But the hole could of been made with a sharp pencil or pen. (or so it looked to me). I took the fastest route possible, the M-C freeway in southern Ontario, within sight of

the water seperating the country's
at times. Speed limit—70 mp.h. I
did over 90 once or twice—danger
gave me an erection. There are no
speeders in Canada. Gas is about 55
cents a gallon—the bargain places
offer 42^9 regular. A can of oil is
$1 & up. The right front wheel gave
me no trouble. I detoured into
Toronto for a rest (me & the car)
and lunch. A friendly gas station
attendent let me go a few cents
better of him—something Americans
just don't do. Saw a lot of
hippie-types in London—an earlier
gas stop. Beautiful shirt sleeve
weather in both towns. Very friendly
people, I think expesaly if they see
you are an American. And about the
only way they can tell is by your
car liensense plate. I had a small
fear that my .38 would go off &
kill some one driving behind me.
And that my Browning would go off
& make a nasty hole in my car.
Unfounded.

It was about 230 miles across
Michigan. About 450 thru Ontario to
Ottawa. I think I left the Howard
Johnson's about 10 am & arrived in

Ottawa thru highway 16 about 9.
I don't remember turning my watch
ahead. Maybe I did it in the Toronto
resturant. Canadains make the
lousyest apple pie, so dry, you
ever tasted. I must of had my suit
on when I crossed the border because
I had it on when I entered the
Canadian capital looking for the
biggest & best hotel their, the
Cheteau Larior. (something like
that) Got directions their from an
Ottawa gas stastion attendent (I
think every gas attendent I ran into
except in London owned the place)
who didn't have a map of the city.

I found it. Drove right up,
somewhat ashamed of the dents on
both sides of my car & asked where
I park & how I could check it.
Door man sent me to the parking
attendente, who got a bell boy to
take my luggage in. Drove all around
& up & down the parking struture
befor I found ONE emty space way
up on the exposed roof. Wondered if
they were full for the night, a
Monday. (the 10th)

A polite clerk said a Geology
convention was in town untill
Thrusday. (the 13th, Nixon arrival
date & supposed death day) The
American Press covering the trip was
in that hotel too. He confessed he
had 3 more reservations than rooms &
could take no stand-by reservations.
As the best Ottawa has to offer, I
thought Nixon would be staying in
that hotel. I wanted to be close to
him & live it up my last few days.
Using the lobby phone I called the
big places, they were full up too.
I looked around for the bell boy,
no can find, so I saved the tip &
lugged my luggage to my car &
started driving & looking. The
same story EVERYWHERE I went,
nothing in the city limits a clerk
explained to a guy in front of me,
"The whole town is closed down."
I drove to a lot of places in town
that night, nothing. I had now spent
4 hours in town looking for a room,
getting very tired & very much
pissed off. I remmember I said,
"Damn this town! It isn't going to
get me down! It wouldn't stop me."

I retraced my route into the capital
city. Saw some cheap looking little
places just outside the city limits.
I went thru maybe 4 towns without
success. The cheap lousy little
places were even full, the last
restort. I ended up driving 58
miles, 58 MILES, out of Ottawa to
wake up a friendly guy for a room.
I thought I would have to cross
the border to get a room for the
trip. About $9 for a 1/2 way decent
room. I ate a few candy bars the
next morning & drove off for a
headquarters closer to town. Got a
dumpy little runt of a room about
5 minutes from the city limits after
trying 2 places a mile closer to
town. Spent the rest of the day
looking over the town & the airport.
Ate a big dinner (& lunch the next
day) at the airport & asked the
waiter causally after I finished if
the President was going to speak
there. He said no it would be at
another airport! I couldn't find
another large airport on my map.
Watching the local T.V. news closely
& looking around as I drove to the
International Airport I found the

entrence to a Military Airport right
next to the commericial one. He
would arrive here, Uplands Airport.

APRIL 22, 1972

I drove round the place a few times
befor & the day of his arrival. The
T.V. gave his expected motorcade
route, Riverside Road. I drove up
& down it to get familier with it.
The T.V. & papers had said, were
saying, & continued to say that
Nixon was getting the heaviest
surcurity coverage of any President
to visit Canada (& they all did
since 1948). I gathered all of my
things into my car. It was a
driszeling day, cold in the lows
40's, about 2:30. Earlier I had
driven all around town & got lost
for a couple hours. It was
confussing. There aren't a lot of
suberbs close to Ottawa. Once you
get outside the city limits your on
a country road. And in the city I
was forbbided to turn left only
when I desperatly wanted to do just
that. I got off track turning right
to go around blocks. During the
trip, I ended up going across the
bridge to Hull at least twice. "Why
don't they label this fucking street
to Hull Bridge Only?"

69

I tryed to conceal the gun in my rubber boot, it was raining & the puddels were bad in places. I drove to the International Airport & took a couple aspirin & adjusted the bulge in my right boot. I couldn't make it look as flat as the left one. And wouldn't it look funny me bending over & grabbing my boot as the President spoak? I left the boots on & put the gun in my pocket. Fuck it. With <u>the tightest</u> security <u>ever</u> I felt for sure a metal detector would be used on everyone. I thought the rubber of my boot would fool it, I don't know why. Dressed in my vested conservative bussiness suit & overcoat with gun & a tie that was just rediculus for anyone my age, I pulled up to the intersection of the Uplands entrance, the road to Internation, the road to town & a road along side the Uplands airport. This last road was patrolled by cops. I watched as about 4 cars got into the place without too much hassel. I wanted to wait a little longer but didn't want undo attention. I pulled up to the guards.

Asked if I could get in to hear

the President speak. A guy who
looked just like me in short hair
& just showered features asked if
I was a member of the armed forces.
No, I just want to hear him speak.
He said there was nothing for the
general public, would I just make a
U-turn please & he would be going
along this main drag any minute &
I could see him then.

Today I wonder if he checked
military I.D.s. The drivers of the
cars that got thru must of had their
I.D.s ready before they got at the
gate. It seems that way now. From
the very beginning of this plan I
planned to get him at the airport as
he addressed a happy Canadian crowd.
Sercurity was tight because of 12-15
or so deserters organizing a protest
& about the same number of Canadian
pafasists who were planning to
protest his arrival & visit. There's
a lot of tension that Canada is an
American owned & almost governed
colony. I felt a lack of
independence all by myself without
being told this. I was about
ready to ask Canadians about this
when I saw it on the front pages
& in editorials of papers & letters
to the editors & in the names of

bussinesses & everywhere. One of
the political big shots there said,
"Any political party not pro-U.S.
will not win the next election."
Talk about imperialism! Live under
it in Canada then you can talk!

I spent about 2 hours driving up &
down the Riverside road over & over
& over again. Surprised I wasn't
stopped & questioned with my strange
yellow American linsense plate &
easily identifiable dented blue
Rambler. Cop cars, very few, were
parked along the road along Uplands,
not even a fence to divid the
airport from the courious. I could
of walked in but didn't know my
way around once inside. And
binoculars were probably scanning
this area. Three men in reflective
orange overalls & carrying
flashlights (it wasn't really dark
yet) searched the road the
President would travel for bombs,
wires strange diggings near by etc.
I guess. Had heard that snowbanks
were watered down to nothing to
destroy a hiding place for bombs.

Saw some men with hoses, cleaning
the street He would use. Watched
the news closly to stay on top of
things.

<u>All</u> the homes & bussinesses
along the route were questioned by
Secret Service men & asked to be
on the look out for strange
movements in the bushes, strange
cars etc. I saw a trench coated
guy, an obvious SS cop, leave a home
along the route & go into his car,
he looked at me as I passed him.

Royal Canadian Mounted Police,
RCMPs, the locals call 'em were
parked or standing at every
intersection & along some train
tracks intersecting the route. A
train could get thru any armored
car! I had parked in a near by
residential area, a couple different
ones to rest & think.

Pulling up from a side street I
asked a fat cop in orange traffic
control vest where a good place
was to watch the President. He
pointed to a empty gas station at
the corner. I thanked him & pulled
in. A few cars were there befor
me & had the choice places. I pulled
behind them & had a good view of
the road 'till more cars pulled in.
Maybe 10-12 cars in all. A young
handsome cop with a moustach took
down all the liesens plate numbers
of the cars coming into the lot.
Anything to keep busy I guess.

It was a long wait. 40 minutes at least, maybe over an hour. Some cops on bikes roared by people got out of their cars & went to the curbless, sidewalk less road. I joined in.

Falsh alarm. Stayed out of the car 10 minutes, fingers got nume. That wouldn't do. I went back in & turned the heater on, still listening to the radio for news flashes. Earlier, I had seen the emty President's Lincoln Continental & all his cops & cars going in to the Uplands base. Against ten-of-thousands of people & tens-of-millions of dollars . . .

I had worn a 3 inch "Vote Republican" button & a 3 inch "Richard Nixon (with his picture)" button to watch the motorcade. I exchanged looks at the Mr. Moustache, my gun inside my pocket. Fantasied killing Nixon while shooting right over the shoulder of that cop.

Came out & went inside again. Longjohn weather. I was conscience of my hands. Didn't want to keep them inside my pockets & get searched. Didn't want to keep them out & nume them too much. Some folks there kept their hands in their pockets almost all the time,

they weren't questioned & either
was I. But I wanted to be
careful, didn't know if a stop &
frisk law existensed or what my
rights were as an American here.
Felt added confidence with my suit
on & short hair & shave.

Didn't recognize my self clean
shaven at first. My head hair came
in nice & thick.

People jumped from their cars.
Would the assassin get a good view?
Everyone moved in close (about 20
people). We were the only people
other than cops for a few blocks.

He went by befor I knew it. Like
a snap of the fingers. A dark
shillowet, waving, rushed by in the
large dark car. "All over", someone
said to no one in particular. The
following cop cars had 2 antentenas
each & probaly walkie-talkies
too--jam proof communications.
Umbrella in one hand, pocket in the
other, I walked back to my car. I
had missed him that day. The best
day to make the attempt was over,
I thought.

Mr. Moustache stopped cars from
leaving the lot too soon--possible
joining the motorcade. Fatty in
the orange vest stopped cars too.
A neatly run operation.

The news the next day said there
were very sparse unwaving crowds.
Said the rain stopped some
demonstrators from showing up to
protest his arrival. All along the
fucking Ottawa visit I cursed the
damn "demonstrators". Sercurity was
beefed up--overly beefed up--because
of these stupid dirty runts. To this
day I blame them for partial
responsibility in failing my
attempt.

I started back toward my cheap
motel. Realized that I had checked
out & today was Thrusday--the
fucking Geologists (I kept asking
myself "What the fuck is a
Geologist", as I carryed my baggage
to the parking lot of the Chateau
& all thru the next day) & that
city rooms would be availiable.
The Chateau was filled with another
convention--I wound up at the Lord
Elgin about 4 blocks away from my
first choice. Nice decent place.

Next few days are a little cloudy
in my mind. I'll have to stop now
& think.

I just ate lunch & took a nap.
It's about 3 pm & I was up at 6
this morning. (Yesterday too)
Nixon spoak at the Parilment to
the Parilment that night. Protesters
were there. I was in my hotel &

getting my first close look at
downtown Ottawa.

Cops had beracades set up in front
of the American Embassy, across
the street from Pariliment. Nixon
was staying at Government House--
a place where the opposition leader
lives at government expense. I can't
remember what Nixon did or where he
went Friday. Let's see--I toured the
National Gallery of Art--an
excellent show house of the work of
the masters if only because there
are more guards then gallery
visitors. Vandalism & graffiti do
not exist there. Frank Lloyd
Wright's building at our own Lake
Front is something else again.
I locked my gun into my carry-on-bag
& put it into my hotel closet as
I had always done befor. I lunched
in the Hotel (eating only 1 or 2
large meals a day all thru the
New York, Canada & Washington
trip--to save time & because
travel food did not really agree
with my guts. But I'm ahead of
myself) walked around & ran into
the Art Gallery 2 blocks away. Not
being sure if I would ever have a
change to get Nixon in Canada after
missing him on my prime target
date, I killed time inside. Some

good mind-expanding work. On a
"closed" floor (no exhibits) I ran
into a male & female guard sitting
& chatting. The guy in a dark blue
uniform, the girl, a blond, in a
light blue miniscrit uniform the
female guards all wore. Sitting in
the middle of the place on a small
seat with the girl the guy walked
all the way over to me (me in my
square suit) & kicked me out (I
could see myself I was lost). Then
he walked back & continued the
romance. Waiting for the elevator
a guard-boss came into the place
& the lovers bounced up & apart
like they had springs in their
asses. "Just talking", the girl
explained. Both of 'em acted real
guilty about something. Bet you
there engaged by now. And fired.

Out of the Gallery I walked down
Sparks Street, shopping area were
cars are prohibited. A woman, middle
age gave me an anti-war/anti-Nixon
leaflet. I glanced it over & handed
it back to her, politely. What could
I say to her? You stupid bitch stop
this useless accomplish-nothing
form of protest, let the sercurity
slacken & I'll show you something
really evective? Tons of leaflets
have been handed out all over the
world for years & what did they get

done? Wipe your ass with this you
radical commie? I support the
President?

She was dressed decently. The
hippie-types also tryed to give
me this stuff, I looked away &
walked on. Wonder what they would
of done or thought of me if they
could read my mind?

Were the cops really afraid of
these people?! Was Nixon afraid,
really scared, of them?!

They're nothing. They're the new
establishment. To be a rebel today
you have to keep a job, wear a suit
& stay apolitical. Now T H A T ' S
R E B E L L I O N !

APRIL 23, 1972

I walked from Sparks St. right on
to the main drag with the American
Embassy on one side & Pariliment on
the other. Ottawa Police formed a
line between the sidewalk & the
Embassy, about 50 cops. About 3
city blocks were cut off to
traffice, pedestrians only. And
farther green barracades prevented
them from crossing the street
without going around additional

barracades. SHOCK! SHOCK! I saw
what I took to be the President's
car parked directly in front of the
Embassy! Was he inside? Wasn't
scheualed to be & WHY would he be
in there?

I went immediately home, ran part
of the way. It was about 15 to
2 p.m. when I got to the hotel. I
stupidly took time to, I'm now
ashamed & embaressed to say, brush
my teeth, take 2 asperin & I think
change from a salt & pepper knit
suit into my black bussiness one. It
was about 2:30 either when I left
my room or when I arrived at the
Embassy.

Car gone.

I had planned to get him as he
entered the car. Saw about 6 white
trenched coated (thought that was
only in the movies!) SS men in front
of the place with the car there.
Less men with the car gone. Weather
the front of the Embassy was used
as a mere parking place (as I now
believe) or BIG SHOT was inside I
don't know. I took my time in the
hotel room because he had made me

wait so long for him on Riverside
Road. I didn't want to attrack too
much attention standing near the
barracade for so long waiting for
Nixon. And I was concerned, overly
concerned with my appearence &
composure after the bang bangs. I
wanted to shock the shit out of
the SS men with my calmness. A
little something to be remmered by.
All these things seemed important
to me, were important to me, in my
room.

I will give very little if ANY
thought to these things on any
future attempts.

After all does the world remember
if Sirhan's tie was on straight?

SHIT, I was stupid!!

Maybe my above time reference was
wrong. It could of been about 10:00.
No! I remember having lunch & very
slow service about 10 that Firday
morning. Anyway I spent all Firday
afternoon outside Pariliment. Saw
the Prime Minister's car (took it
to be Nixon's) go into the grounds.
Saw Nixon waveing (wife beside him)
being driven up into the grounds ten

minutes or more afterward. Started
up a conversation with an Ottawa
cop & he said they would talk about
an hour. This period (exact times)
is foggy in my mememory.

An RCMP in ceromonial uniform
turned me away from getting in to
the grounds. I saw other people get
in a little latter thru this &
another entrence. I used the other
entrence, past a gas fed flame
straight up to the steps leading
into the West Block of Pariliment.
The place was swarming with people.
Mostly people who had been at the
steps leaving. A few, like me, went
in the other direction. I made my
way as close as the public was
allowed. Less than 30 people were
with me. I was a little concerned
over the lack of Canadian concern.
We were held back by a green
barracade & about 15 real pretty
RCMP's in ceromonial uniform. They
looked pretty enough to top a
wedding cake, to the street, 100
yards behind, a red flag & banner
carrying crowd & a guy with a bull
horn yelled & marched. They marched
up to & on to the steps just befor

the mounties dyed of boredom. They
had been shifting their feet an
awful lot with nothing to do. Small
conversations between groups of 2's
were broken up went 300-400 shouting
people marched in. THAT woke up the
Little Dolls!

Mr. Bull Horn bounced his voice
off the building with a couple dozen
"Nixon Go Home"s. He turned to
address the crowd. Some other guys
spoke too. A wild shouting idoit
shouted some senseless phrases. The
kind of guy Hollywood hires to play
the wagon train attacking Indian.

All speakers were heckled by 3
sick looking hippies, Heroin maybe.

After awhile it appeared the only
protestors were the guys holding the
red flags (2) & the banner (2) &
Mr. Bull Horn (5 all together). A
guy tapped me on the shoulder.

"RCMP", he says. He looks like
any body.

He goes in front of me & carefully
photographes the speakers.

What a dope! Those noise makers
were all on news film! He should of
photographed the quiet ones. He
never pointed his camera at me.

Looking back at the crowd, I saw
2 SS men (they were SO! easy to
find) at each side at the foot of
the stairs.

The crowd pressed close to the
barracade. I had to be careful not
to let anyone press against my right
coat pocket and feel the outline
of my noise maker.

The nuts tryed to get thru the
barracade. Pushed back at once.
More loud speaker talk. Too much
noise for me, Nixon would never
come up to shake hands with such a
crowd, the one thing I hoped he
would do at some time during the
trip.

I walked back to the gas fed
flame, 20 feet from the street. A
number of the 400 curious had
walked back here for quiet. Earlier
a Lincoln Continental had come &
went from another door. The PM or
just an empty decoy. 100 Ottawa
cops in a double line formation
jogged from the building to the
gate. Waving again, Nixon was driven
past me the 2nd time that day.

After a pause, the crowd was
allowed to get lost. Looking up, I
noticed earlier 2 SS men with
binocculars on top I think it was
the Embassy. I waved & looked
directly at one of 'em to mock
their whole fucking sercurity
systems. I felt stupid afterwards
when he looked right at me thru
great big binoculars for minutes on
end. Or at least till I had crossed
the street & gotten to far under
him for him to see me at all.

I walked past the Chauteu, a
little further on, & turned back for
my room. That night Nixon went to a
concert in his honor at the
Performing Arts Center, 1 or 2
blocks from the Lord Elgin. A white
tie affair for 2,000 by invitation
only. I walked around the joint any
way on my way to dinner at the
Chauteu. Later it turned out that a
political big shot was turned away
by a mistaken Mountie. To wear white
tie & tails & get Nixon-boy, WOW!
If I killed him while wearing a
sweatty tee-shirt, some of the fun

& Glamore would defionently be
worn off.

Had a big Manhatten, straight,
& an $11 meal at the Chauteu that
night. $1 for pea soup alone. Salads
were $2, I feared a meal in itself
& didn't order any. Maybe vegatables
(& fruit--orange juice in
particular) are just expensive this
far north. Had an expensive steak--
always do when eating out. Was
sitting their still woozy from
the drink--maybe I had two of those
things. Wanted it over ice, had
said, "Manhatten--over," but what
happened I don't know. Maybe ice is
expensive this far north.

I went back to the bar. Another
one of those things. Watching the
band, the people talk, the people
dance, the bar maids, watching the
people watch others. No desair
to talk. Canadians drink a lot of
ale. Ale bottles everywhere.
A guy came in & asked the
bar-keep for a drink to take back
to the press room. Ice-less said it
was against the rules. A short
argument. The reporter lost.

"Thats Canada for you," I said.

"It's not Canada, its just this (pointing to bar-keeper) fucking cunt!"

Walks quickly away.

"A _fucking_ cunt is the best kind of cunt to be," I say to the amusement of a fat man in glasses.

I give my bar stool up to a guy so he can sit with his girl, after I took my time finishing my drink. An effort needed to walk straight, but less than needed after dinner.

About the press room. I had seen signs in the Chautau lobby pointing out the "White House Press Room" & a lot (25 maybe) typewriters & people in their. Earlier I had seen a ceremonial Mounty in tails & they (cops) all had a private party in a rented hall just off the hotel lobby. Couldn't join the party, didn't have the tails. Left my gun locked up for dinner.

Strolled into the press room like
I belonged their. Read a
blackboard & some papers on a
corkboard. Only one thing
useful. A note giving Nison's
time schual for Saturday morning.
When leave Gov. House, when arrive
west block Parilment, when leave
Parilment, when arrive Uplands
Airport. And the press people were
to have their baggage ready "at
8:50 am NOT 9:00 am." I wrote it
all down. The papers & T.V. had not
given this out so detailed. A woman
& man reporter (appeared to be
together) came up behind me &
complained about the early baggage
call. I felt I found out about all
I could from the place so I left.
People were coming in from the
concert.

Asked to be awakened at 7 am &
thought that I would be too tired
& hung over to get up but I was up
at 6:30 checking my notes & washing
up and writting a real long sentence.

Had seen Nixon driven from the
Arts Center on my way home. Walked
around the place. A ceromonial
Mounty greeted me "hellow, sir" &
we talked a little.

"Well, I guess its all over for you for today. Tomorrow afternoon you can relax again."

"Yeah. I'd like to relax. I've been working for the last 16 hours straight."

We parted. I was thinking that if he worked that hard, I should be working at least as hard. At this time I also began to think of following Nixon to Washington. Was about 1 am went I went to bed. Had a little admiration just then for Nixon. He must of been retiring about the same time. Was schualed to leave Gov. House at 9:10 am, but he could sleep on the plane. I planned to meet him at 9:25 at the Parilment. He would sign a Great Lakes Pollution treaty (without reading it himself) & arrive at Uplands 10:10 am.

I didn't try to get into the Parilment grounds. There weren't enought people there for my taste. I hung around the front of the Embassy. Walked past the 100 other cops & dozen SS men with my gun. A small accomplishment I thought.

Off to the left the protestors a
large shouting mass, stronger &
larger looking than Friday's petiful
group, had pushed its way thru a
driveway & marched up to the
building. It seemed to surprish the
cops & SS. Some men began to go
over there. They were called back,
"Let 'em thru." A new "hold" line
closer to the building was set up.
I was so busy trying to look
saddened & concerned that they had
gotten thru, I couldn't feel any
satisfaction that sercurity had
broken down under a harmless group.

It started to rain lightly. I
entered a hallway allready occupied
by a small 30tish woman, "You got a
good place here," I said. She
mumbled something. I turned to face
the street & a trench coat stepped
into the doorway obviously blocking
my freedom of movement. It didn't
occur to me at the time he wanted
out of the rain too. Maybe he did.
Yet I didn't want to be held in the
doorway sultically or not when His

car went by. A commotion on the left
got him out of my way. I left the
cubby hole right away.

Nixon was leaving. He was driven
out a gate just 20 yards or so to
my right. The sparse crowd in front
of the Embassy ran off to that gate.
The SS & cops were in confusion. "Is
he coming out?" "That gate?" A
garboled voice came over the
walkie-talkie I moved close to hear
& then he came out. About as far
away from the protesters as he could
get. The Ottawa cops, SS, & Mounties
formed a line to hold back the
crowd. I had a good view as he went
past me, past me again, the 6th
time & still alive.

I knew with the sparse friendly
crowd, the protesters making noise
& the rain he wouldn't show himself
for a succesful attempt. Waiting
for him to come out that last time
I even thought of killing as many
SS men as I could. Because I was

pissed at them & myself & Nixon
killing 5 or 6 Secret Service
agents would get me in the papers
SOMETHING to show for my effort.
Killing 'em right in front of
Nixon--dig it!? I wasn't sure my
flat tipped .38's would go thru the
bulletproof glass. Didn't want to
get emprisoned or killed in an
unsucessful attempt. To have
absolutely nothing to show--I
couldn't take that chance.

Somewhere along the line--Friday
or Saturday I got photographed by
an SS man, I'm sure of it.

I was walking across Sparks Street
& noticed a white trench coat
crossing behind me, not looking at
me no but awfully funny he should
decide to cross the street the same
time I did & just 15 feet behind
me. I surely didn't think he was
off duty! Shit! was he stupid or
was I? He even stopped to look at
the same window display as me.
Then he carelessly walked ahead to
the very next window. I stayed wore
I was. He returned to my window &

walked around on the other side
of me (again out of his way). I
looked right at him innocently,
he looked at me. He was tall, 6"3'
brown hair, thin features, looked
like a cop. A cop trainee. A cop
trainee who flunked out. I continued
to looked behind him & saw another
trench coat aimming a 16 mm camera
at me. I looked up the street.

There was nothing in that
direction to photograph. Nothing
for an SS man to be interested in.
Even a tourist (in a white trench
coat, with a professional camera,
with a careless pal) would not
photograph something void of
interest. I was certain the lens
was pointed right between my eyes.
Maybe that was it . . .

The big guy was to get me to turn
right into the lens so SS could have
a photo (& witness) & say "this man
was in Ottawa when Nixon was."

I turned the corner & lost track
of the big fella. Walked in circles
for a while & then back to my
room--back to another surprish.

APRIL 24, 1972 MONDAY

I sure now I was photographed
Saturday, in the late morning. I
guess their were right to do it. I
had hung around there all alone &
for a long time--too long to be
innocent. Later I thought it would
of been cute to do a Charlie
Chaplin walk & twist my hat around
my index finger & lift up a leg &
spin around for the great movie
maker. Maybe even call out to the
Big Fella, "Hey stupid! I'm leaving,
come on!" And walk up the street.
They would of shit in their pants.
Dropped the camera in surprise.
Foulded for the exposed roll of
film bouncing out of the camera &
gone chasing it like a couple of
Keystone Cops. "Trench Coat Home
Movies, Inc."

At my room I considered going
home or going to Washington. Figured
Ottawa was closer to D.C. than
Milwaukee was, why go to Milw.
when I might end up in Washington
a little later anyway? Can't kill
Nixy-boy if you ain't close to him.

It took forever to check out.
Exchanged 5 Canadian twenties
for 5 U.S. twenties at the Hotel.
He wouldn't take any more. Had
about $450 I gues--ain't sure at
all. Packing my cloths (I can't
spell a thing) I noticed the lock
on my carry-on-bag was tampered
with. It looked as though some one
had put some thing into the key
hole & turned it, creating a very
noticablly enlarged key hole. My
key was now too small to fit the
hole. I further enlarged the hole
in order to get into my own bag.
Nothing was gone. I don't think I
had anything in there. Previously
I kept only my gun, ammo & a salt
& pepper knit suit in there.

Now, all during my stay at the
Lord Elgin I kept the T.V. or radio
on--loud enought to be heard at the
door--the lights near the door on,
and a "Do Not Disturb" sign on the
door whenever I was not in my room.
Enought stuff to stop a less
determined sneak thief. My room
was cleaned with a "Do Not Disturb"
sign on the door knob.

The bell captain said--no, a lot of burglaries had not been reported in this hotel--what else could he say without losing his job. The manager said--too confidently--that no one had been in my room--how the fuck could he be so sure?--but the maid. I told him the 3 precautions against theft I had taken. No, nothing was taken but would you take not of this & if it happens again you know it happened befor.

Thoughts of the Secret Service-- the always somewhat clumsy & confused Secret Service--haunted the back of my brain. If the hotel was co-operating with them--& why wouldn't they?--the SS knew my name, address, linsense plate & that I lissted the M.A.C. as my employer. A phone call to them & they knew I was unemployed. All together enought little tid bits to question me.

Maybe it was the maid, maybe the SS, maybe it was just me the day befor nervously & aniously going for my gun to return to the Embassy. But I don't remmember being nervoius, being calm--super cool--was very important to me.

A determined punk could of cut thru
the bag with a pen knief. Why did
he just try to pick the lock? The
metal was very soft & palitable.
It could of given way (bended)
befor a lock picker knew it. The
attache case, with perhaps a
somewhat better lock, did not
appear tampered with.

That lock is still a mystery. I
don't think he got it opened.
Tryed--saw the hole he made &
stopped.

Could it of been just
photographed?! HA, HA.

APRIL 24, 1972 TUESDAY

Shit! I am thruorly pissed off.
About a million things. Was pissed
off befor I couldn't find a pen to
write this down. This will be one
of the most closely read pages since
the Scrolls in those caves. And I
couldn't find a pen for 40 seconds
& went mad. My fuse is about burnt.
There's gona be an explosion soon.
I had it. I want something to
happen. I was sopposed to be Dead

a week & a day ago. Or at least
infamous. FUCKING tens-of-1,000's
of people & tens-of-millions of $.
I'd just like to take some of them
with me & Nixy.

A L L   M Y

                E F F O R T S

                        &

                                N O T H I N G

C
H
A
N
G
E
D

Just another   god Damn

failure

Oh man, I a werewolf now changed
into a wild thing. I could give it
to the fucking mayor really fuck
his little machine. Burn all these
papers & what I buried & no one
would ever know 1/2 of it.

But I want em all to know. I want
a big shot & not a little fat noise.
I want that god damn
   tired of writting about it.
   about what I was gonna do
   about what I failed to do.
   about what I failed to do again
& again.

Traveling around like a hobo or
some kind of comical character.

I'm as important as the start of
WWI I just need the little opening
& a second of time. Nothing has
happened for so long, 3 months, the
1st person I held a conversation
with in 3 months was a near naked
girl rubbing my erect penis & she
wouldn't let me put it thru her.

FAILURES

Goddamn news man on the radio
says the weather today sounds "like
a polition we all know when he
says, "Let me make this perfectly
clear".

All the news this week has been
about the S. Viets losing the war
& the space shot. Nothing left for
the primaries & Nixy in Moscow
May 22-29. Fucking rain & cold all
the time since I came back. Was
warmer in Canada.

Every thing's wrong I'm even a
week behind in my writing. (Ha Ha.
Maybe I need a vacation!)

THERE ain't one leaf on any tree
in this fucking city. Had
temperatures in the upper 20's
last night, the fucker on the radio
said the western suberbs could
praise god because their high
would be 54 today. 54 Shit!

EVERYTHING Shit

Had bad pain in my left temple
& just in front & about it. Kept
me awake for a--seemed a long time
last night. Remember I had at least
2 night mares last night. Bad
frieghtening dreams--that's a
night mare ain't it? I allmost
never dream & now when I did it
was terrible. Didn't want to
remember them long enought to write
them down either then--was I 1/2
awake?--or at a later time. Forgot
'em pretty well now.

Everything drags on . . . drags
on . . . and on . . .

It was supposed to be all over
now. Don't think I have enought
money to pay the rent on the 15th
next month & eat that month too.
I gota get him. I'm tired, I'm
pissed, I'm crasy. Was gona get
drunk last night--WOW--what a
personality change. Decided against
it--just wanted to pick a fight with
the bartender some where or
someone. Get arrested & then where
am I. I got something to do--
something big befor I ever get
arested again.

Tired of writting, writting, a
<u>War & Peace</u>. Emphasis on the war.
I keep throwing my pen. It won't
be a nice composed vested suited
man--it will be a mad man who kills
nixon & he will kill him he will be
dead. I go crasy with delight when
I hear Jhonny Cash's new record,
"<u>You Put me Here</u>".
      "I shot you with my .38
      And now I'm doing time"
Weather is shit. Called off a ball
game for the rain. Called off
another for the cold.

I'm back to writting. May 4, 1972
Thursday. 10 days have passed since
my last entry. And even then I was
a week behind in writting things
down. Had to get away from it for
a while. Needed some fresh air &
exercise.

When I came back up untill my
last entry, I morned my failures &
stayed indoors--back to the exact
same existence I had as befor the
trip. Everything was the SAME
except I had less money. Much less.

I had to get away from my thoughts
for a while. I went to the zoo, the
lake front, saw "Clockwork Orange"
& thought about getting Wallace all
thru the picture--fantasing my self
as the Alek on the screen come to
real life--but without "my
brothers" & without any "in and
out." Just "a little of the old
ultra violence."

I've decided Wallace will have
the honor of--what would you call
it?

Like a novelist who knows not
how his book will end--I have
written this journal--what a
shocking surprise that my inner
character shall steal the climax and
destroy the author and save the

anti-hero from assasination!! It may
sound exciting & fasinating to
readers 100 years from now—as the
Booth conspricy seems to us today;
but to this man it seems only
another failure. And I stopped
tolerating failure weeks ago.

As I said befor, I Am A Hamlet.

It seems I would of done better
for myself to kill the old G-man
Hoover. In death, he lays with
Presidents. Who the hell ever got
buried in 'Bama for being great?
He certainly won't be buryed with
the snobs in Washington.

SHIT! I won't even rate a T.V.
enteroption in Russia or Europe
when the news breaks—they never
heard of Wallace. If something big
in Nam flares up I'll end up at the
bottom of the 1st page in America.
The editors will say—"Wallace dead?
Who cares." He won't get more than
3 minutes on network T.V. news. I
don't expect anybody to get a big
thobbing erection from the news.
You know, a storm in some country
we never heard of kills 10,000
people—big deal—pass the beer and
what's on T.V. tonight.

I hope my death makes more sense
than my life.

A few days ago I felt sick--a
slight fever & hot feeling in my
chest, sides, & back. A sharp
pinprick moving pain in left temple.
Headacke. Weakness in my heart.
And a feeling like a cool wind was
moving in my hands. The pain in my
temple stayed a few days. Yesterday
I went to see the Milwaukee
Techinacal Colledge Photography
Department's show at Capital Court,
ignored the shops. Unexpectedly, I
felt such a sharp pinprick moving
pain in my left side, I thought I
would fall to my knees & then fall
some more. I stood still & then
walked slowly--like an old man--
with only a hint of the pain left.
The rest of the day, I took it easy.
WHAT THE FUCK WAS THAT!? In my left
side above my lower ribs.
    It helped, I think, to hold my
breath & then take only shallow
breaths.

Still feel--& have for a while--a
general weakness in my heart.

The whole country's going liberal.
I can see it in McGovern. You know,
my biggest failure may well be
when I kill Wallace. I hope everone
screams & hollers & everything!!
I hope the rally goes mad!!!
May the 16th is primary date in
that beautiful state across Lake
Michigan--Michigan. Wallace is
believed to be strong there. He'll
have a rally in Detroit. I'm sure
of it, once this week's primaries
are over.
I wish I could give it to the
Nixonites who crossed over and
made Wally-boy look strong with
over 300,000 votes in Indiana. A
recurring fantasy of mind is to kill
50 or so cops & dicks in unmarked
cars in this little community. I
hate those unmarked cars & I can
spot 'um anywhere.
I passed some time in Milwaukee's
misdemenor courts--would like to see
a falony trail but I have to spend
all next week in Michigan on
bussiness.

Soda water radio commercial says, "You gota lot to live". My anwser, "Yeah, about a week."

Just got back from seeing "Z.P.G." & "Such Good Friends" (by Otto Preminger). Probaly the worst picture he ever made. Jennifer O'Neil was great but the female lead was serious during the jokes & jokeious during the heavy parts. Z.P.G. had a piece that should of been shortened (an endless boat ride thru a sewer), but really hit home with people playing with dolls, paste-food, super-smog, etc.

"Good Friends" was as bad as "Vixen" by Russ Mayer. Dog shit with a plastic flower in it.

Funny . . . I've got nothing to say.

Have I ever said anything?

I only hope someone other than a peace officer, persecuter, judge & jury read this. But right now--I don't know why.

MAY 8, SATURDAY

Yesterday got books about Sirhan Sirhan, "R.F.K. Must Die!" a Warren Commission like report by Robert Blair Kaiser & an unread as yet dumpy looking "Sirhan", by Aziz Shihab. I think he's a fake & a phony.

Gotta leave soon.

I'll stay here long enough to eat all the food up.

Still don't know weather its trail & prison for me or--bye bye brains. I'll just have to decide that at the last few seconds. Must secceed. Gota.

As late as yesterday I had thoughts of burying this whole paper & reading it decided later after I had gone to Hollywood (I KNOW IT SOUNDS INSANE, SO DON'T THINK IT)

& making my fortune on the old
sivler screen.

Sure! The same way I was gonna
fuck 4 million of New York's finest.

That empty page awhile back
represents my morning of lost
information. Like I said I got
pissed & didn't write for awhile.

Crossing the "Bridge to America"
I took a great drive--with thrilling
manificent views thru some N.Y.
mountains. Got a speeding ticket I
didn't yet mail back to a judge.
Then ran into a fog so thick I (in
a hurry) slowed from a legal 60 to
10 m.p.h. at times. At 45 I thought
it was more exciting than a roller
coaster. I couldn't see the front
of my car hood. I steered by the
white line in the middle of the
road & then a cop stoped me again
because I was slowing traffic that
wanted to pass! I drove about 250
miles thru that night fog. Got into
Washington 4-6 hours behind the
scheual I set for myself, 4 AM
instead of Midnight, earlier with a
tail wind.

I was pissed at losing my
Browning 14 shot & missing the Big
Bastard so I went thru American
customs with the .38 in my coat
picket. (suit on) I had lost all
respect for "customs". A fat timide
guy who either sucked his thumb or
bite his nails looked in my trunk.
He said, "OK", almost befor it was
fully opened.

The first cop told me my right
rear turn signal didn't work. Later,
after honking at & passing a
Milwaukee cop car I was ticketed
for a burnt out tail light. (It had
poped out of its socket I found out
later. And replacing the turn
indicator (in side the car) would
cost $14. I used hand signals.)

I thought I was in D.C. but was
in Callotsville Md.--something like
that--& was gona spend the night
parked in a dark corner at a
shopping center parking lot untill
daylight. My reservation at Howard
Johnson was nonexistent. The clerk
sounded like he didn't want to be
bothered. A real nice guy at some
other place, 300 rooms maybe, was

full up too. Then a guy checked out
& I was called back. A room in 15
minutes! But the clerk, after an
inspection, said it would take an
hour or so to clean up the real bad
mess that guy left behind him. I
was directed to the Sheraton N.W.,
& they charged me a whole day
checked in after 4 am (out time 1
p.m.) But the guy their gave me a
real big nice room at the bussiness
rate of $17 per instead of 20. I
said a 2 week stay, it was only 3
days.

I was about 20 miles from D.C. &
another 20 from the White House.

He never made an apperence for me.
But had a big party the night he
returned with an opera signer (big
tits stuckup nose & all). Man I
thought he had it good. One party
after another for 4 years.

I left. Cheaper maybe to pay my
rent $138.50 for 30 days rather
than $17 per. I could drive back if
anything required my presence.

And you know something? Our great
leader made an appearnce in front
of the White House to shake hands
with tourists the day after I left!

I was planing to be ther that day
but wanted to use the the day light
to drive by. I never got in the
building--Closed to vistitors on
Sun. & Mon. & I goofed off Tue.

Saw a photo of his hand shaking
--man he was right there! So close!
I tore the whole paper to shreds.

I could of killed him for doing
<u>that</u> alone.

I left a shitty waitress a 2¢
tip, two Canadian cents! Had a $5
meal.

You know America doesn't have to
be imperialistic. She allredy owns
the free world by reasons of
economics. Compare the G.N.P. of
US with all of Europe. Japan sends
what? 50% of its stuff over hear?
If America sneezes doesn't everyone
say, "gonsunhdit?" Everyone in the
leadership of Britain, Phillipines,
Canada, all South & Central America
& Viet Nam lock stock & barrel.

One example. In Canada the vending
machines accept American & Canadian
coins. In America the machines do
not & to make it perfectly clear a
large decal commands, "Do Not Use
Canadian Coins".

In Canada, U.S. coins are accepted as currency by machine & people.

An internation bank in D.C. exchanged my $4 plus in small Canadadian coins at 85¢ on the dollar.

We save our military imperialism for those areas not under our economic imperialism. But what bothers me is why do the factory owners--the rich--support all of our wars? Guess the rich get richer and the poor get shot.

Passed the last week or so fasinated with storys in the papers discussing murder, suicide & the death penalty. Disapointed that Michigan doesn't have death penalty. But I remember from High School that a man can drownd on one drop of water. I think I could do it if I held my head back & jaw open & quickly dropped an ounce of water down my throat without swallowing. Right into the windpipe --bypassing the food tube. I have other more realistic plans for that kind of stuff. I won't write this down.

I was afraid that 1st cop would
ask me to step out & then pat
me down. But I was NEVER in N.Y.
befor so I had no record, there. I
hid the gun in my umbrella close
enought to use, & I would of befor
he called my name & car make in, if
I needed it. He was a real nice guy
thou. The umbrella reminds me it
also rained & hailed on top of the
fog as I traveled down the east
coast. I was really tired pulling
into what I thought was Washington.
But the weather there, ahh. . . .

I was overjoyed with the warm
sunny weather. I kept shouting in
happiness, "It's summer!" Temps in
the 70's tee shirt weather. And
grass! And leaves on trees! Pure
green grass 3 & more inches high.
(Not cut yet from winter I thought.)

Back in Milw., the beatiful
trampled into the ground brown hay
was another world.

I took the toll roads from Washin.
Soon as I went 200 feet on my last
toll way, I took a wrong turn &
went 20 miles back the wrong way.
40 miles total. I was trying to

drive & read the toll ticket at the
same time! My smooth right front
tire scraed me at times. I slide in
turns & took forever to slow down
or stop. Had it changed in
Milwaukee. Thankful it held out.

And I was thankful--to nobody in
particular--to be back in Milwaukee.
Shouted & yelled as I drove across
the Wis. border untill I made my
first stop--the landlord's office.
Wasn't in.

His handy man caught me in the
laundry & I had to pay him. Didn't
want to get kicked out or in
cop-trouble but wanted to hold onto
my precious few remaining funds.
Thought I'd be leaving again in
days, weeks at the most.

Had thrown a lot away but didn't
miss it when I didn't have it to
morne over.

Felt like an utter failure.

Two-hundred-forty-one pages--WOW!
I should of been dead about 60 or
70 pages ago. This paper probaly
would of made more sense then.
Most of what I write now is blah.
The main theme has left it.
    I understand the principle of
"less is more". And:

    I tried to fuck Lady-Luck
    But she locked her knees
    And wouldn't please
    The wedding cake
    Arrived too late
    And now we have to call the whole
        thing off.

    She has a sister
    And she will screw
    I'll race her engine
    My penis made me
            do it.

Hey world! Come here! I wanna talk to ya!

If I don't kill--if I don't kill myself I want you to pay thru the nose, ears, & belly button for the beginning of this manuscript. The 1st pages are hidden & will preserve a long time. If you don't pay me for them, I got no reason to turn 'em over--understand punk!?

One of my reasons for this action is money and you the American (is there another culture in the free world?) public will pay me. The silent majority will be my benifactor in the biggest hijack ever!

It was kidnapping in the early part of this century. Then hijack became popular with sky diving a often time extra added attraction.

I'm gonna start the next crime binge! HA. HA. And the silent majority will back me all the way!

Irony!!
Irony!!

SUNDAY MAY 7, 1972

There's les than a hundred pages
in my "unhidden" journal. I was
about right--60 to 70 pages ago was
to be one of those days "which will
live in infamy" & all that.
Yesterday I even considered McGovern
as a target. If I go to prison as an
assissin (solitary forever & guards
in my cell, etc.) or get killed or
suicided what difference to me? Ask
me why I did it & I'd say "I don't
know", or "Nothing else to do", or
"Why not?" or "I have to kill
somebody".
   That's how far gone I am.
   Often I've thought of just turning
this whole manuscript over to a
welfare (can I spell it?)
pyscologist & asking for his
opinion.
   NURSE! GET THE JACKET!
   If you think you need a doctor I
guess you're

It bothers me that there are about 30 guys in prison now who threatened the Pres & we never heard a thing about 'em. Except that they're in prison.

Maybe what they need is organization. "Make the First Lady A Widow, Inc." "Chicken in Every Pot and Bullet in Every Head, Com., Inc."

They'll hold a national convention every 4 years to pick the exacutioner. A winner will be chosen from the best entry in 40,000 words or less (preferrably less) upon the theame "How to Do a Bang-Up Job of Getting People to Notice You" or "Get It Off Your chest; Make Your Problems Everybody's".

My heart again. Just after getting
out of bed this morning. I bent over
to put a leg thru my pants, felt a
heavy intense pain over a large
area of my left upper back. Tryed
to put my pants on again. Same pain.

After straightening up & a few
seconds time lapse, I noticed it
came from behind my heart & I
thought in front of my left lung.
These arteries are called the
pulmonaries I think.

One thing for sure, my diet is
too soft. Weakens my posture maybe
affects my insides too. I am one
sick assissin. Pun! Pun!

I really feel releaf in my back
when I lay on the floor. Regarding
everything else; suicidal thoughts
have been known to generate physical
symptoms. Guess only my generator
is healthy.

Read about 1/2 of Kaiser's book.
Really like it. A good man with a
pen.

Hard to feel any heart beat. It's
very dull & shallow. Who would think
an assissin weak hearted?

Really would feel better if
Michigan had a death penaty. The
trial might be interesting but after
the visits from the attorneys and
how will I spend my time in my
little cell?

You know, suicide is a birth
right.

I dreamed last night. Forgot it.

I just remembered something. When
I flew back from N.Y.C., I ate at
the usual resturant I eat at when
I'm in a hurry. A counter girl
recognized me & asked, "Did you
just inherit a million dollars or
something?" I was so surprised (I
didn't see her at first as someone
else waited on me) that I made her
repeat it, "Did you just inherit a
million dollars or something?"

Then I realized how happy I was to
be going to Canada (the boat would
leave for Michigan in a few hours
& I was sure I would get him & I
thought about my staying at the
Waldorf & that messuse). I admitted,
"Yes, something."

I was always her biggest grouch
before that.

Recalling that reminds me further;
Diana Ross was at the Waldorf (as a
performer). I didn't want to see
her because I felt she had watered
down her talents for the rich
whites--broadened her appeal and
narrowed her ability.

A Gray woman--you know?

Found something to do with my $10
Confederate Flag. Wiped the dust off
my shoes with it befor polishing
them. It's too thin to use as a
polish cloth. "Wish I was in the
land of cotton." Bang! 'Bama.

I'm gonna get convicted. It's
gonna be very similer to Sirhan.
Might as well flaunt the fucker.
on second thought, fucking's too
good for him.

"Shot you with my .38 and now
I'm doing time. You put me here,
you put me here."

I'll take the 3 am boat over the
lake in 11 1/2 hours. Damn weather
is the low 40's with clouds and
rain. Can see the exhaust vaporize
from tailpipes. Need a coat.

Hope he doesn't keep me waiting.
Like I said, I could of gotten him
6 weeks ago. I'm absolutly sure of
that. His agents are liberals.
Wanna bet? It'll come out in court.

Or an inquest after my death.
It all depends on how things go.

Abortion/Orgasm/and Holy Cow

When you're a fetus
The joys & tortures & boredoms
Of life
Are beyond your wildest dreams.
And who among the living
Can say they, once us, don't
    dream?

I wonder if
The joys & tortures & boredoms
Of death
Are beyond your wildest dreams.
And who among the dead
Can say they, once us, don't
    dream?

MAY 13th, 1972 SATURDAY

Well I made it across the Lake.
Ship left about 4 a.m. Didn't sleep
too well. Got out of bed to see us
sail past the break water & in to
the sunrise. Arrived about noon.
Was stopped on Highway 10 (all cars
were) by a cop for "vehical
inspection." He looked at my driving
lincese & said, "Expires in 1972."
That was my inspection.
   Ate in Saginaw and read its paper.
Wallace was allready in the state
for a few days. Next rally--Dearborn
that night at 8:00. It was near 3
pm when I left. I started a frantic
mad run for Detroit to ask
directions to Dearborn--a suberb.
Went into a black owned & run gas
service station & asked directions.
I made him repeat it 3 times so I
could be sure. I thought, was
certain, he said John C. Lawrence
freeway. He was saying John C. Leary
or something like that. Went past
it 5 times looking for the Lawrence
freeway. I wound up at Coks Hall &
was lost again. Finally found
Dearborn. Pulled in for a can of oil
& changed into a suit & tie. It was
about 5:30. Loaded my .38. Couldn't
find the belt for my pants. "Excuse

me sir, is this your gun?" Adjusted
the gun many times that night.

Arrived at Dearborn Youth Center
at 15 after 6. Was lucky to find
a parking place on a "Not Thru
Street."

The hall was packed & 1,000 or
so waited outside ahead of me.
Papers said 3,000. I say 2500
inside; 2,000 outside. The speaker
said a second rally might be held
at 9:15 if enought people remained.
Later I read they had done this in
Flint & another city. Wallace talked
'till 9:35 & no second rally "Since
the sound outside was so good."
Yeah they had speakers. I did the
best I could. Asked a cop sargent
ordering all the other cops around
were we could get in for the 2nd
show, "which door do we use."

"Second show tonight? No, I don't
think so.

If I couldn't be 1st in line for
the second show, I'd be near the
entrence door for Wallace. There
were windows on the sides of the
hall & some people the lucky ones,
had a view into the hall to see
what they could hear. You had to
stand up on a ledge to see. A
make-shift "backstage" area was
formed by blue curtains seperating
the back door from the inside

audience. People at the 2 window
panes closest to the door could,
however, see all unobstructed.
"Allways somewhat careless," I
thought of the S.S. The thin glass
was weakly reinforced with wire
mesh. But no trouble for a bullet
at all. That was my plan.

When Wallace appeared behind the
curtain we "supporters" went wild.
Crys of "I see him. I see him. There
he is. He's right here". He
delighted in "our" enthusiasum.
Came over to wave hello twice. Then
came over to ask if we could hear
the singers over the outside
speakers. He used sign language.
Exposed himself 3 more good times
for this--a glorified Junior High
School Audio-Visual Aid. He took
the podium. We at the window could
see him thru a crack in the
curtains.

As he spoke demonstraters marched
around outside--now were inside.
Guess they got there late too.
"Wallace & the Klan go hand in
hamd." "Stop Wallace. I spit as
I walked past 'em to my choice
viewing position. Had to wait a
long time for someone to step down
so I could get up there.

Dearborn cops carry mace behind
their .38's & 2 1/2 foot clubs, the

longest I had ever seen up till
then.

A teen age girl behind me said
she could shoot him thru the curtain
crake. She was joking about her
intentions. A guy said something
against Wallace. I was going to ask
him who he would want to be
President but decided to forgo the
philosophy dicusion & wait for my
opening. Half a dozen kids watched
in near by trees.

He talked & talked. The ranks
outside thined. Not even many at
the windows. I cursed. I wanted
him to wave at us & come close as
he left. He gave a couple cinema
men some good "Wallace & supporters"
shots. I wanted my shot to. Did the
Secret Service men really think a
piece of glass was a deterent? Not
to me! I was all set. Jacket
opened. A still cat befor he
springs. Waiting . . . Waiting . . .
He's left the podium!

He took less time to wave good-bye
then he did to wave hellow. And he
didn't come right up to the glass.
15 feet instead of 5 feet away.
No proden but . . .

Two 15 year old girls had gotten
in front of me. Their faces were 1
inch from the glass I would shatter
with a blunt-nosed bullet. They were

sure to be blinded & disfigured.
I let Wallace go only to spare
these 2 stupid innocent delighted
kids. We pounded on the window
together at the governor. There'ld
be other times.

I was low on money & wanted a
cheap place to spend the night.
Drove past a place called the
Capital or the Congress Motel. The
name sign must of cost 'em 3
thousand dollars alone. Too
expensive. Drove on down the street.
No other places. Drove on down the
street. No other places. Drove
back to the Congress Inn.

A cop didn't want me to park next to
the building. "Park over there,
around the corner instead." I told
him I just wanted to check in. I did
what he said. Took the .38 from my
pocket & put it under the seat.
   Asked a reporter, as easy to spot
as a SS "You got big doings around
here?"
   He was bored, "Governor Wallace
is staying here," as if to say
"No nothing big."
   Jackpot!
   The cop was stationed right outside a room, curtains open, full of
his strategy people in conference.

That's were I first parked.

No vacantcies. Got a reservation
at another joint. Asked the sargent
at the door how to get there. Good
directions. A good cop. I like a
good cop.

Got tired of driving the 6 miles
to the place thou & stopped at a
cheaper joint. Thought I was lost
againt but was 7 blocks from my
reservation. The girl who took my
reseration never told me the name
of her motel. All I had was a street
corner. So I said fuck it & stopped
at Allen Town (a city I think) &
slept there.

Morning paper said he'ld be in
Cadillac, Michigan at 8 that night.
Drove back the way I had come twice
befor. (1) Nixon & (2) Wallace in
Dearborn & stoppped in Clare to eat
a big lunch. My last meal as a free
man I thought. Really surprished my
self that I left 1/2 of everything
on my plate. Veal cutlet--mashed
potatoes--applesauce (I ate all of
that)--& apple piece a là mode--
milk (all of it). Took a couple
asperin. Tried on a pink pullover
sweater to see if it would cover
the .38 on my waist. It didn't.
Wanted to wear something different
than I wore in Dearborn. All the
wail Wallace talked, his SS men, the

ones behind the curtain goofing off
smoking a pipe (a dark serious guy)
& a couple others downing sodas,
got good looks at me. And Caddilac
is a long ways off from a Detroit
suberb. On my way out saw a couple
Detroit cops frisk down a couple
guys in the road. Thought for sure
if the SS saw me in Caddilac, they
would feel justified in asking me a
few questions. "Following us?" "I
just wanna see the Governor," sir."

Arrived in Caddilac well ahead of
time. Found out were the High School
gym was from a drive in. The local
paper & the radio told me to look
for the gym. Except for some unpaved streets (on hills mostly), I
liked the town. I guess with snow
& ice unpaved streets are best on
hills.

In Dearborn a kid pointed out
"Police Chief O'Riley." A nice
looking guy. I imagined myself
apologising to him & cheering him up
with, "Don't blame yourself for the
lack of surcurity blame the Secret
Service." I would of told him that
had I been succesful.

I would see plenty of local big
wigs in Caddilac. It was a really
beautiful day. I drove around the
gym & parked near a lake. Layed
down & relaxed with a paper over my

face. Had to piss. Had plenty of
gas. Had plenty to eat. Where to go?
A bar. Had 2 Manhatins. Drank 2
glasses of water. The drinks didn't
bother me much at all. Except
financialy. A buck each. Nice little
bar. Good bar tender. I thought of
Sirhan. He had 4 drinks & was, he
claimed drunk, when he did his
thing. One of the songs the female
organist sang touched me. Forget
what it was.

The mayor or some political
bigshot came in & all rised their
glasses to him. He said he
introduced Wallace to all the local
big shots & took plenty of time
doing it. Wanted to be on the local
T.V. that much longer. "I never
knew I was a ham!" He broke up the
crowd. That was at the airport.
Two hours ago. On the news that
night I watched as he shook hands
with every one & his brother over
the airport fence. A fence is
surcurity? I would be relaxing in
jail & not running all around trying
to catch him now if I was at the
airport.

I left for the rally. Arrived at
6:15 behind a crowd of 125 or so.
I knew I was late when I left the
bar. Smalled talked with the shit
head next to me.

The same singers. The same songs.
Two SS men flank the stage on each
side as Wally talks, center stage
behind his usuall high bullet-proof
podium. More agents flank the crowd
& the stage entrence. Bored
gargoyles. Unmoving. Unemotional.
Searching. One with a coat on his
lap. Rifle inside? I am, at the very
most, 35 feet from my target. In
the 5th row. Too far to risk. Need
a sure shot. I am the most
enthusiastic hand clapper for the
songs & the spech. Want him to feel
comfortable. The crowd isn't as
responsive as in Dearborn.

I want to get closer. "Shake Hands.
Shake Hands," I cry. No. He has to
go to New York from here tonight &
with the time zone change & yak
yak. At the end of the speech, I
try to push the people in front of
me & in my row forward or out of
the way so I can get close. No
luck. A dozen big shot behind
Wallace were introduced as being
for him--mayors of hamlets &
other guys. Yet why wasn't this
crowd responsive? I DID THE MOST
HAND CLAPPING, ALL THE SHOUTING, &
WAS GOING TO START 3 DIFFERENT
STANDING OVATIONS BUT FELT THE
CROWD WOULDN'T FOLLOW ME.

I bet He didn't want to shake
hands with them! No cheers or speech
interruptions! A great
disappointment for him I bet. Poor
guy. What would he have done
without me?

It took me 3-5 minutes or more
to get out of the building. These
SS men are a different crew than
was in Dearborn. No suspisions.
Wallace was not out of the area
yet! Another security breakdown.
And no cops to hold back the crowd
from stepping in front of his
following cars.

He was driven out, I got a look
at him, in a Caddilac (what else?).
Must of shook hands with people
outside to cause the delay. Or he
talked with his people & some
reporters befor he left. The car
was moving when I saw him & didn't
know if he was on the left or right
side rear seat. Dark in the car of
course. If it stopped . . .

After all, who ever heard of a
bullet proof Caddilac?

The following cars were stuck
behind. A smart agent opened his
door wide to sweep people away. A
nice trick. Almost too late. But
almost doesn't count.

I walked to my car swearing,

swearing, swearing. Spent the night
in Caddilac. Amost 10 o'clock. Too
late to drive. Too tired. Too
pissed.

He'ld be back in 3 days to cover
Jackson, Kalamazoo, & Lansing the
capital of Michigan.

Drove to Lansing. Read its papers.
Drove around it. Drove right out.
Demonstrators again! Shit! Against
the mining of N. Nietnam. Shit!
If it wasn't for demonstrators
4 weeks ago . . . No mining.
Remember Ottawa! TRA-TAAAA!

Cops in East Lansing had
positively the longest clubs I
ever saw & they needed 'em. All
4 feet of 'em. The kids had
barakaded a street. Lots & Lots
of cops & cops in riot gear. A
place to avoid without a second
thought for what I had in mind.

Went to Jackson. Then read it's
paper. Headline "Jackson Cancelled
for Warren". Considered going back
to Warren--a Detroit suberb really
hard to find on my map. Said a
"downtown" rally. "Outside?"
Something different. Saw him talk
outside on T.V. in Escanoba or
Marquette. I favored an indoor
rally. His schual was Warren at 3
& Kalamazoo at 8. If I went to one,
I couldn't drive to the other &

get a good close seat. I considered
alternatives very carefully.

He wanted to go to Warren
cancelled Jackson for it.

He was well treated in another
Detroit suberb.

Warren was outside. Kalamazoo
inside. I would have to fight all
of Detroit to get a good seat in
Warren. Kalamazoo wasn't so
populaeded.

When I heard that 1/2
of the states votes were in the
Detroit area, I decided right then
to go to Kalamazoo & meet him there.

A short drive from Jackson. I
stayed at a hotel overlooking the
Kalamazoo National Guard Armory
where he'ld talk. Watched it
carefully. Wanted everything
perfect. Paper said 10% chance of
rain Sat., today, afternoon. I'm
checked out of my room & sitting
in my car now & writing & its
raining like a son-of-a-bitch.
Will this spoil everything?

Was _very_ warm yesterday. This
morning I could smell rain in the
air. He'ld talk at a $25 plate
dinner. Then at the Armory,
capacity 2,300. Then leave for
Maryland tonight for 2 days of

campaning. They have a primary the
16th too.

He drew 4-6,000 in '68 at a near
by city Park. Read the paper in the
beautiful mall area of town.
Listened to rock music, in a park.
A small ineffective protest is
planned today.

Wanted to be the 1st in line.
Thought I saw people standing in
front of the place at 9 this
morning. They moved on. Rain is
letting up slowly now. It's about
1:30. He isn't in Warren yet. But
I'll soon be on the front steps of
the Kalamazoo Armory to welcome
him. Got a sign from campaing
headquarters here. To shield the
go for the gun.

Is there any thing else to say?

My cry upon firing will be,
"A penny for your thoughts."

Ottawa, Ontario

1. Need birth certificate for
   Canadian entry
2. Copy of the car rental
   contract &
3. a Canadian customs form to leave
   a rented car in Canada.

Biggest hotel (or motel) in Ottawa,
Ontario is the Chateau Laurier
Hotel (515 units) next to War
Memorial, Conferation Square,
overlooks Pariliament Building &
Rideau Canal and the Art Center.
Air conditioning, color TV--radio.
Single $16-$22. indoor pool, sauna
& Turkish bath. Phone (613)
232-6411. Resturant 3-$7.50. 7 am
to midnight, not the best food.
Try the Embassy, 60 Bank St. at
Sparks St., shisk-kebab & steaks.
The Butler Motel for food. Lroo
Tavern Dining Lounge, 201 Queen St.
Tourist season is May-September.

Editor's Note

Two days later, in Laurel, Maryland, Arthur Bremer shot George Wallace. Bremer was wearing sunglasses and a red, white, and blue shirt decorated with Wallace buttons. At least one witness remembered that as Wallace left the speaker's rostrum, behind which he had been shielded by bulletproof glass, Bremer cried out: "Hey George! Hey George! Over here!"

Later that same day the newspapers reported that a search of Bremer's room in Milwaukee had uncovered, among his other possessions, a Confederate battle flag, a gun catalogue, and a pornographic comic book. He apparently had no friends. The few people with whom he had been acquainted described him as being timid and withdrawn. Somebody said he had wanted to become a writer or a commercial photographer, somebody else remembered that his mother had refused to let him try out for the high-school football team. Otherwise the record remained pathetically incomplete, the blank spaces suggesting the vast loneliness of a life condemned to impotence and failure.

When the judge pronounced sentence, Bremer, in response to the traditional question as to whether he had anything to say, remarked: "Looking back on my life, I would have liked it if society had protected me from myself." On August 4 of last year he entered the Maryland Penitentiary in Baltimore. He has appealed the verdict of the state court, and he awaits trial in a federal court on various charges of interfering with an election and violating George Wallace's civil rights.